First World War
and Army of Occupation
War Diary
France, Belgium and Germany

15 DIVISION
Divisional Troops
71 Brigade Royal Field Artillery
3 July 1915 - 31 May 1919

WO95/1923/4/1

The Naval & Military Press Ltd
www.nmarchive.com
Published in association with The National Archives

Published by

The Naval & Military Press Ltd

Unit 10 Ridgewood Industrial Park,

Uckfield, East Sussex,

TN22 5QE England

Tel: +44 (0) 1825 749494

www.naval-military-press.com

www.nmarchive.com

This diary has been reprinted in facsimile from the original. Any imperfections are inevitably reproduced and the quality may fall short of modern type and cartographic standards.

© Crown Copyright
Images reproduced by permission of The National Archives, London, England, 2015.

Contents

Document type	Place/Title	Date From	Date To
Heading	WO95/1923/4		
Heading	15th Division 71st Brigade R.F.A. Jly 1915-May 1919		
Heading	15th Division "B"/71 Battery R.F.A. Vol. I From 8th To 29th July 1915		
War Diary	Bulford	08/07/1915	08/07/1915
War Diary	Southampton	08/07/1915	08/07/1915
War Diary	Harve	09/07/1915	10/07/1915
War Diary	Audruick	11/07/1915	11/07/1915
War Diary	Polincove	11/07/1915	14/07/1915
War Diary	Lynde	14/07/1915	15/07/1915
War Diary	Mollingheim	15/07/1915	16/07/1915
War Diary	Lapugnoy	16/07/1915	20/07/1915
War Diary	Vermelles	20/07/1915	29/07/1915
Heading	15th Division 71st Bde. R.F.A. Vol I Jly-aug.		
War Diary	Bulford	03/07/1915	08/07/1915
War Diary	Havre	09/07/1915	10/07/1915
War Diary	Audruicq	11/07/1915	11/07/1915
War Diary	Polincove	12/07/1915	15/07/1915
War Diary	Lynde	15/07/1915	16/07/1915
War Diary	Molinghem	16/07/1915	17/07/1915
War Diary	Lapugnoy	17/07/1915	29/07/1915
War Diary	Mazingarbe	30/07/1915	29/08/1915
Heading	15th Division B/71 Battery RFA Vol 2 Aug & Sep.15		
War Diary	Philosophe	27/08/1915	27/08/1915
War Diary	Vaudricourt	27/08/1915	27/08/1915
War Diary	Vermelles	05/09/1915	26/09/1915
Heading	War Diary Headquarters, 71st Brigade. R.F.A. (15th Division) September (29.8.15 To 30.9.15) 1915		
War Diary	Mazingarbe	29/08/1915	20/09/1915
War Diary	Philosophe	19/09/1915	25/09/1915
War Diary	Loos Road Keep	26/09/1915	26/09/1915
War Diary	Quality Street	27/09/1915	30/09/1915
Heading	15th Division 71st Bde. R.F.A. Vol 2 Oct 15		
War Diary	Quality Street	01/10/1915	03/10/1915
War Diary	Mazingarbe	04/10/1915	31/10/1915
Miscellaneous	15th Division. 9.10.15 Special Divisional Order	27/09/1915	27/09/1915
Miscellaneous	Special Order Issued With 15th Divisional Routine Orders Of 16.10.15	16/10/1915	16/10/1915
Heading	15th Div 71st Bde. R.F.A. Vol 3		
War Diary	Vermelles.	01/11/1915	17/11/1915
War Diary	Gosnay.	18/11/1915	22/11/1915
War Diary	Annequin	23/11/1915	30/11/1915
Heading	15th Div. 71st Bde. R.F.A. Vol. 4		
War Diary	Annequin.	01/12/1915	16/12/1915
War Diary	Auchel.	14/12/1915	16/01/1916
War Diary	Mazingarbe	17/01/1916	31/01/1916
War Diary	Mazingarbe	01/02/1916	29/02/1916
War Diary	Mazingarbe	01/03/1916	31/03/1916
War Diary	Mazingarbe	01/04/1916	16/04/1916
War Diary	Ames	17/04/1916	29/04/1916

War Diary	Noyelles.	30/04/1916	30/04/1916
Operation(al) Order(s)	Left Group Operation Order No. 1.	27/04/1916	27/04/1916
Operation(al) Order(s)	71st Brigade RFA Operation Order No. 5	27/04/1916	27/04/1916
War Diary	Novelles.	01/05/1916	31/05/1916
Heading	War Diary Left Group 71st Brigade R.F.A. 15th Divisional Artillery HQ. 71 Bde. RFA. ABC & D/71 B & C 170 D/73 & 1/2C/73. May 1916		
War Diary	Novelles.	01/05/1916	31/05/1916
War Diary	Novelles.	01/06/1916	30/06/1916
Heading	War Diary 71st Bde R.F.A. From 1st to 31st July, 1916.		
War Diary	Novelles.	01/07/1916	22/07/1916
War Diary	Anvin.	23/07/1916	25/07/1916
War Diary	Monchel	26/07/1916	26/07/1916
War Diary	Dutrebois	27/07/1916	30/07/1916
War Diary	Bethencourt	31/07/1916	31/07/1916
Heading	War Diary 71st Brigade R.F.A. 1st-31st July 1916		
Heading	15th Divisional Artillery. 71st Brigade. Royal Field Artillery August 1916		
Heading	War Diary of 71st Brigade R.F.A. From 1st August, 1916 To 31st August, 1916 Volume Number 14		
War Diary	Bethencourt	01/08/1916	02/08/1916
War Diary	Begecourt	03/08/1916	03/08/1916
War Diary	Albert	04/08/1916	04/08/1916
War Diary	Caterpillar Valley	05/08/1916	08/08/1916
War Diary	?	09/08/1916	14/08/1916
War Diary	Near Montantarn	15/08/1916	31/08/1916
Heading	War Diary of 71st Brigade, Royal Field Arty. From 1st September, 1916 To 30th September, 1916 Volume Number 15		
War Diary	N. Montauton.	01/09/1916	29/09/1916
War Diary	Contalmaison	30/09/1916	30/09/1916
Heading	War Diary of 71 Bde R.F.A. 1st October, 1916 To 31st October, 1916. Volume. 16		
War Diary	Contalmaison.	01/10/1916	17/10/1916
War Diary	St Gratien.	18/10/1916	26/10/1916
War Diary	Bazentin Le Petit.	27/10/1916	31/10/1916
Heading	War Diary of 71st Bde R.F.A. From 1st November, 1916-30th November, 1916. Volume 17		
War Diary	Bazentin-le-Petit	01/11/1916	14/11/1916
War Diary	In The Field.	15/11/1916	30/11/1916
Heading	War Diary of 71st Brigade R.F.A. From 1st December, 1916 To 31st December, 1916 Volume 18		
Miscellaneous	15. D.A.	31/12/1916	31/12/1916
War Diary	Bazentin Le Petit	01/12/1916	12/12/1916
War Diary	Pierregot	13/12/1916	24/12/1916
War Diary	Lower Wood	25/12/1916	31/12/1916
Heading	War Diary of 71st Brigade R.F.A. 1st January 1917-31st January 1917 Volume 19		
War Diary	Lower Wood.	01/01/1917	31/01/1917
Heading	War Diary of 71st. Brigade R.F.A. 15th. Divisional Artillery For Month Of February 1917 Volume XX		
War Diary	Lower Wood	01/02/1917	04/02/1917
War Diary	Mirvaux	05/02/1917	15/02/1917
War Diary	Outrebois.	16/02/1917	16/02/1917
War Diary	Ligny-sur Canche	17/02/1917	17/02/1917
War Diary	8 Michel	18/02/1917	22/02/1917

War Diary	Arras	22/02/1917	28/02/1917
Heading	War Diary of 71 Bde R.F.A. From 1st March 1917-To 31st March 1917 Volume 21		
War Diary	Arras.	01/03/1917	31/03/1917
Heading	War Diary of 71 Bde R.F.A. Volume 22 From 1st April 1917. 30th April, 1917		
War Diary	Arras.	01/04/1917	09/04/1917
War Diary	H 26.b.	10/04/1917	11/04/1917
War Diary	Feuchy.	12/04/1917	23/04/1917
War Diary	Near Monchy 7. at NIIa 5.2	24/04/1917	30/04/1917
Heading	War Diary of 71st Brigade R.F.A. From 1st May, 1917 To 31st May, 1917 Volume 23		
War Diary	Near Monchy At N 11 A 5.2	01/05/1917	21/05/1917
War Diary	Arras.	22/05/1917	23/05/1917
War Diary	Hazarcq	24/05/1917	24/05/1917
War Diary	Etrge Wamin	25/05/1917	25/05/1917
War Diary	Boubers Sur Canche	26/05/1917	31/05/1917
Heading	War Diary of 71st Brigade, R.F.A. From 1st June, 1917. To 30th June 1917. Volume 24		
War Diary	Boubers Sur Canche	01/06/1917	15/06/1917
War Diary	E.P.S.	16/06/1917	16/06/1917
War Diary	St Hilaire	17/06/1917	17/06/1917
War Diary	Steen Becque	18/06/1917	19/06/1917
War Diary	Eecke	20/06/1917	20/06/1917
War Diary	Watou	21/06/1917	30/06/1917
Heading	War Diary of 71st Brigade R.F.A. From 1st October 1917. To 31st October, 1917 Volume 28		
War Diary	Athies.	01/10/1917	31/10/1917
Heading	War Diary of 71st Brigade R.F.A. Volume 28 From 1st November 1917. To 30th November 1917		
War Diary	Athies	01/11/1917	28/11/1917
War Diary	Feuchy	29/11/1917	29/11/1917
War Diary	Feuchy H 23 C5090	29/11/1917	30/11/1917
Heading	War Diary of 71st Brigade R.F.A. Volume 29 From 1st December 1917 To 31st December 1917		
War Diary	N Fampoux H 23 C 5090	01/12/1917	04/12/1917
War Diary	Nr Fampoux	04/12/1917	26/12/1917
War Diary	Ins Fampoux H 23 C 5090	27/12/1917	31/12/1917
Heading	War Diary of 71st Brigade R.F.A. Volume 30 From 1st January 1918 To 31st January 1918		
War Diary	Nr Fampoux	01/01/1918	04/01/1918
War Diary	Arras.	05/01/1918	31/01/1918
Heading	War Diary of 71st Brigade R.F.A. Volume 31. From 1st February 1918. To 1st March 1918		
War Diary	Arras	01/02/1918	07/02/1918
War Diary	Wiry Corner	08/02/1918	28/02/1918
Heading	15th Divisional Artillery. 71st Brigade R.F.A. March 1918		
Heading	War Diary of 71st Brigade R.F.A. (Volume 32) From 1st March 1918. To 31st March 1918		
War Diary	Airy Corner	01/03/1918	22/03/1918
War Diary	Wilderness Camp.	23/03/1918	24/03/1918
Miscellaneous	71st Bde R.F.A.	25/03/1918	25/03/1918
War Diary	Wilderness Camp.	28/03/1918	28/03/1918
War Diary	Cemetery. Arras.	29/03/1918	31/03/1918

Type	Description	From	To
Heading	15th Divisional Artillery War Diary 71st Brigade R.F.A. April 1918		
Heading	War Diary of 71st Brigade R.F.A. (Volume 33) From 1st April 1918. To 30th April 1918.		
War Diary	Cemetery. Arras.	01/04/1918	04/04/1918
War Diary	Arras.	05/04/1918	30/04/1918
Heading	War Diary of 71st Brigade R.F.A. (Volume 34). From 1st May 1918. To 31st May 1918.		
War Diary	A.C.Q.	01/05/1918	04/05/1918
War Diary	Rollincourt	05/05/1918	31/05/1918
Heading	War Diary of 71st Brigade R.F.A. (Volume 35) From 1st June 1918. To 30th June 1918.		
War Diary	Roclincourt	01/06/1918	17/06/1918
War Diary	Ecurie.	18/06/1918	20/06/1918
War Diary	St. Nicholas	21/06/1918	27/06/1918
Heading	War Diary of 71st Brigade R.F.A. (Volume 36.) From 1st Aug. 1918. To 31st Aug. 1918		
War Diary	St Nicholas.	28/06/1918	22/07/1918
War Diary	Chazelle	23/07/1918	26/07/1918
War Diary	Chazelle Valley	27/07/1918	31/07/1918
Heading	War Diary of 71st Brigade R.F.A. From 1st August 1918. To 31st August 1918. (Volume 37).		
War Diary	Chazelle Valley	01/08/1918	02/08/1918
War Diary	Dommiers	03/08/1918	03/08/1918
War Diary	Barberie	04/08/1918	04/08/1918
War Diary	Sarron	05/08/1918	05/08/1918
War Diary	En Route Frevent.	06/08/1918	06/08/1918
War Diary	Berlencourt.	07/08/1918	17/08/1918
War Diary	Arras.	18/08/1918	31/08/1918
Miscellaneous	Hqrs 15th Div. Confidential.	30/09/1916	30/09/1916
Heading	War Diary of 71st Brigade R.F.A. (Volume 38) From 1st September 1918. To 30th September 1918		
War Diary	Vis-En-Artois	01/09/1918	08/09/1918
War Diary	Mazingarbe	09/09/1918	30/09/1918
Heading	War Diary of 71st Bde R.F.A. From 1/10/18 To 31/10/18 Volume 39		
War Diary	In The Field. at G 17.b.93	01/10/1918	05/10/1918
War Diary	G. 7b 93	06/10/1918	10/10/1918
War Diary	Philosophe	11/10/1918	15/10/1918
War Diary	Meurchin	16/10/1918	16/10/1918
War Diary	Ennecourt	17/10/1918	17/10/1918
War Diary	Martinval	18/10/1918	18/10/1918
War Diary	La Capelle	19/10/1918	19/10/1918
War Diary	Genech	20/10/1918	20/10/1918
War Diary	La Glanerie	21/10/1918	22/10/1918
War Diary	Rue du Hotel	23/10/1918	31/10/1918
Heading	War Diary of 71st Brigade R.F.A. (Volume 40). From 1st November 1918. To 30th November 1918		
War Diary	Rucd'Hotel	01/11/1918	08/11/1918
War Diary	Petit Rumes.	09/11/1918	09/11/1918
War Diary	Braffe	10/11/1918	10/11/1918
War Diary	Aubechies	11/11/1918	30/11/1918
Heading	War Diary of 71st Brigade R.F.A. (Volume 41.) From 1st December 1918. To 31st December 1918		
War Diary	Aubechies Chapelle A Oie	01/12/1918	16/12/1918
War Diary	Chievres	17/12/1918	17/12/1918

War Diary	Horrues	18/12/1918	18/12/1918
War Diary	Rebecq-Rognon	19/12/1918	31/12/1918
Heading	War Diary of 71st Brigade R.F.A. (Volume 42) From 1st January 1919. To 31st January 1919.		
War Diary	Rebecq. Rognon	01/01/1919	31/01/1919
Heading	War Diary of 71st Brigade R.F.A. (Volume 43) From 1st February 1919. To 28th February 1919		
War Diary	Rebecq-Rognon	01/02/1919	28/02/1919
Heading	War Diary of 71st Brigade R.F.A. (Volume 44). From 1st March 1919. To 31st March 1919		
War Diary	Rebecq-Rognon	01/03/1919	31/03/1919
Heading	War Diary of 71st Brigade R.F.A. (Volume 45) From 1st April 1919. To 30th April 1919		
War Diary	Rebecq-Rognon	01/04/1919	30/04/1919
War Diary	Rebecq	01/05/1919	31/05/1919

WD95
1923(4)

15TH DIVISION

71ST BRIGADE R.F.A.
JLY 1915 - MAY 1919

15th Division

121/6508

"B"/71 Battery R.F.A.

Vol: I

From 8th to 29th July 1915

Army Form C. 2118.

WAR DIARY
or
INTELLIGENCE SUMMARY.
(Erase heading not required.)

Instructions regarding War Diaries and Intelligence Summaries are contained in F. S. Regs., Part II. and the Staff Manual respectively. Title pages will be prepared in manuscript.

Place	Date	Hour	Summary of Events and Information	Remarks and references to Appendices
BULFORD	8/7/15		Marched off	
SOUTHAMPTON	8/7/15		Embarked	
HAVRE	9/7/15		Arrived	
HAVRE	10/7/15		Entrained	
AUDRUICQ	11/7/15		Arrived	
POLINCOVE	11/7/15		Marched to Billets	
POLINCOVE	14/7/15		Marched off	
LYNDE	14/7/15		Billets	
LYNDE	15/7/15		Marched off	
MOLLINGHEIM	15/7/15		Billets	
MOLLINGHEIM	16/7/15		Marched off	
LAPUGNOY	16/7/15		Billets	
LAPUGNOY	20/7/15		Rx Marched off	
VERMELLES	20/7/15		Rx Attached 114 Battery for instruction	
VERMELLES	24/7/15		Lx Attached 114 Battery for instruction	
VERMELLES	29/7/15		Rx + Lx joined up and took over gun position of 16th Battery (London Territorial) BETHUNE—LENS road 10° fire zone. North from	

1577 Wt. W10791/1773 500,000 1/15 D. D. & L. A.D.S.S./Forms/C. 2118.

121/7153

15th Division

7ot Bde: R.F.A.
Vol I

Ju. Aug. & Sept /15

a/s
a/s

Page 1

71st BRIGADE. R.F.A.

Army Form C. 2118.

WAR DIARY
INTELLIGENCE SUMMARY
(Erase heading not required.)

Place	Date	Hour	Summary of Events and Information	Remarks and references to Appendices
	July			
BULFORD	3-7-15	9.0pm	Received orders to hold ourselves in readiness for immediate embarkation overseas.	
do	4-7-15	8.0am	Telegram received stating 13th Div'l Artillery would start embarking on 5th July. Advanced officers to go to-day.	
do -	8-7-15	12.15am	71st Brigade R.F.A. started entraining at AMESBURY Station to proceed to SOUTHAMPTON. Brigade Ammunition Column went first in 3 separate trains. This was followed by B. C. D + A Batteries + Bde Headquarters. ½ a Battery went in one train. ½ A Battery with Bde Headquarters left AMESBURY Station at 1.15 pm. The last train of 71st Brigade R.F.A. on 6-7-15.	
HAVRE	9-7-15	8.30am	Arrived HAVRE + proceeded to disembark. No casualties occurred on the voyage. Disembarkation was completed by about 1 pm + after certain Ordnance Stores were drawn from the A.O.D. units proceeded	

Page 2
Army Form C. 2118.

WAR DIARY
INTELLIGENCE SUMMARY.
(Erase heading not required.)

Place	Date	Hour	Summary of Events and Information	Remarks and references to Appendices
			to Rest Camps as follows:-	
HAVRE	10.7.15	9.0 am	Bde Headquarters to No 1 Camp ST. ADRESSE	
		4 pm	A. Battery " 7 " "	
		1.45	B. " " 5 " Near GARES MARITIMES	
		1 pm	C. " " 1 " ST. ADRESSE	
			D " " 1 " "	
			Bde A.C. " 1 " "	
			B Battery entrained at GARES MARITIMES	
			Bde Headquarters left No.1 Camp with A Battery to proceed to	
			GARES MARITIMES to entrain. Remaining units following at intervals.	
AUDRUICQ	11.7.15	1.0 pm	Train with Bde Hqrs & Battery arrived at AUDRUICQ.	
			Detrained in 30 minutes & proceeded to billets at POLINCOVE	
POLINCOVE	12.7.15		In billets at POLINCOVE. These billets were very good. All horses	
	13.7.15		were in well sheltered fields & men in barns.	
	14.7.15			

Page 3.
Army Form C. 2118.

WAR DIARY
or
INTELLIGENCE SUMMARY
(Erase heading not required.)

Place	Date	Hour	Summary of Events and Information	Remarks and references to Appendices
POLINCOVE	15-7-15	8.30 a.m.	Started to march to LYNDE. Route via NORDAUSQUES – ST MARTIN AU LAERT – extreme SW sheets of ST OMER – ARQUES – WARDRECQUES – LYNDE. This was a divisional march with all troops. The halts were not long enough to allow the horses to be watered or fed.	
LYNDE	15-7-15	3.30 p.m.	Arrived LYNDE.	
LYNDE	16-7-15	10.0 a.m.	Left LYNDE to march to WITTES at MOLINGHEM via WITTES – AIRE.	
MOLINGHEM	"	1.0 p.m.	Arrived MOLINGHEM.	
"	17-7-15	10.0 a.m.	Left MOLINGHEM to march to LAPUGNOY via LILLERS – LOZINGHEM.	
LAPUGNOY	17-7-15	1.30 p.m.	Arrived LAPUGNOY	
	20-7-15	5.0 p.m.	One Section from A Battery joined the 113th Battery 1st Division at VERMELLES for a period of 96 hours. Also one Section from B Battery joined the 114th Battery 1st Division at VERMELLES for a period of 96 hours.	
	24-7-15	5.0 p.m.	The remaining sections from A & B Batteries joined the 113th & 114th Batteries	
	26-7-15	10.0 a.m.		respectively for 96 hrs.

Casualties in B Battery other ranks – 2 killed 2 wounded while digging.

WAR DIARY
INTELLIGENCE SUMMARY
(Erase heading not required.)

Army Form C. 2118.

Page 4.

Place	Date	Hour	Summary of Events and Information	Remarks and references to Appendices
LAPUGNOY	27.7.15	after dark	One section from A. Battery replaced one section of 15th London Bty (6th London Brigade R.A) in action at PHILOSOPHE. This section and its registering on 28th.	
"	28.7.15	"	The remaining section of A Battery on completing of their work 113th Battery replaced the remaining section of 15th London Bty. One section of B Battery on completing 96 hours with 114th Battery replaced one section of 16th London Bty (6th London Bde R.F.A.) at PHILOSOPHE. This section registered on 29th	
"	29.7.15		Remaining section of B Battery at LAPUGNOY replaced the remaining section of 16th London Bty	
"		11.0 am	Bde Headquarters moved to CHATEAU MAZINGARBE. The telephonists came 24 hours before to take over lines &c.	
			Every night D Battery dig from 10.0 pm to 2.0 am - preparing emplacements for their guns to come into.	
			Also the Infantry (Pioneer Btt) send men to each Battery at night to dig a deep dug-out for the use of the detachments.	

Army Form C. 2118.

WAR DIARY
or
INTELLIGENCE SUMMARY.
(Erase heading not required.)

Instructions regarding War Diaries and Intelligence Summaries are contained in F. S. Regs., Part II. and the Staff Manual respectively. Title pages will be prepared in manuscript.

Place	Date	Hour	Summary of Events and Information	Remarks and references to Appendices
MAZINGARBE	30th	5 pm	A/71. 2nd – B/71. The left section repulsed G.28.D.19. & G.28.C.9.5. Also during the night the Battery Bug outs were commenced with infantry working parties	
"	31st	3 pm	A/71 repulsed H.31.D.08.9 at 4.20 pm repulsed G.28.B.45. Also fired in retaliation on G.28.A.6.3 at 7.5 am.	} firing
"		4.30 pm	B/71 Registered G.28.C.9.5 and retaliated at report of infantry on G.28.C.9.1 at 4.50 pm.	
"		11.15 am	The enemy put some heavy shell into Zone 3 and repeated into VERMELLES	} General
"		3.30 pm	Five fatigue parties were observed 1 mile E.N. of VERDIN – report to heavy artillery	
"	1st Sept	8.30 pm	A/71 fired 24 rounds on G.28.6.3.5 at the report of the infantry as the enemy were trying rifle grenades. The enemy stopped immediately.	
"	2 Aug	3.50 am	A/71 fired on G.22.D.8.0. at report of infantry and B/71 on G.34.B.77.	} Tasks
"		11.0 am to pm	A/71 fired on G.22.D.8.0 at report of infantry and B/71 on G.34.B.77.	
"	3 Aug	6.5 am	A/71 fired on front line trench in x.2 zone at report of infantry	
"		10.35 am	A train was observed proceeding towards VENDIN LE VIEL from the direction of WINGLES – it stopped before WINGLES.	
"		11 am	The Wagon lines of A./3 & A/71 moved to DROUVIN – C/71 to NOEUX-LES-MINES – and the B.A.C. to HESDIGNEUL.	

WAR DIARY
INTELLIGENCE SUMMARY

Army Form C. 2118

Place	Date	Hour	Summary of Events and Information	Remarks and references to Appendices
MAZINGARBE	August 3rd	5.50 pm	B/71 fired on front line trench in X, zone at request of infantry	
"		4.45 pm	The firmans who observed to be working in the trenches at G.28.D.19.	Trats.
"	4th	9.30 am	A/71 fired on G.22.D.91 at request of infantry.	
"		3.5 am	B/71 " " G.29.C.93 " " "	
"		8.5 am	A/71 fired in front line trenches in X, zone at request of infantry.	
"		9.50 am	B/73, which came under the command of O.C. 7th Bde RFA at 6 am this morning, fired lyddite into LOOS in retaliation, and it was reported that the enemy burnt the hypo, please CHEVRON de FRISE on large fortification at G.28.B.59. [note. one section only of B/73 is at present in action and is at torre 7.]	
"	5th	8.55 am	A/71 fired in retaliation on G.22.D.80 & G.28.B.31 in retaliation.	
"		9.30 am	B/71 fired 36 rounds at enemy front line trench in G.28.C in retaliation	
"			also B/73 fired lyddite at enemy trenches between G.23.B.38. & G.23.A.43 in retaliation and also into LOOS.	
"		12 noon	B/71 fired on G.28. C.91. in retaliation.	
"		3.30 pm	B/73 fired lyddite in LOOS in retaliation for enemy shelling Fosse 3.	
"		4.30 pm	A/71 and B/73 fired on G.28.B.7.6 where minnie werfen were supposed to Captain McKenzie gone out. C/71 came back into reserve in NOEUX-LES-MINES.	

Army Form C. 2118.

WAR DIARY
INTELLIGENCE SUMMARY.
(Erase heading not required.)

Place	Date	Hour	Summary of Events and Information	Remarks and references to Appendices
MAZINGARBE	Aug. 6th	10 a.m.	B/71 fired on enemy front line trench in x.1.30.u in retaliation	
	"	10.30 a.m.	Smoke at regular intervals and shot towards as if from enemy battery were observed S.W. of Fosse 8.	
	"	12.45 p.m.	A train was seen to emerge from S. of VENDIN-LE-VIEIL and proceed towards CITÉ-ST-AUGUSTE.	
	"	3.40 p.m. till 5.5 p.m.	A/71 fired on LOOS PYLONS, G.26.b.7.2. G.22.d.8.3 & G.23.a.4.3. in retaliation.	
	"	6.15 a.m.	B/71 fired on enemy front line trench in x. zone in retaliation – also at 6.35 p.m.	
	"	5.30 p.m. till	D/73 fired 39 rounds lyddite into LOOS & vicinity of HULLOCH in retaliation	
	"	7.15 p.m.	Two rounds were observed to detonate on house in H.7.C. as smoke was emitted for 4 or 5 minutes.	
"	7th	11.30 a.m.	D/73 fired lyddite at report of infantry into LOOS	
	"	11.30 a.m.	report Fosse 3 was shelled with light & heavy shells & were replied to by heavy battery.	
	"	11.55 a.m.	Information received about working party at H.26.c.5.6, fired lyddite off the map.	
	"	2.40 p.m.	D/73 fires into LOOS in retaliation & at 4 p.m. in retaliation for enemy shelling Quality Street.	

WAR DIARY

INTELLIGENCE SUMMARY

Army Form C. 2118

Instructions regarding War Diaries and Intelligence Summaries are contained in F. S. Regs., Part II. and the Staff Manual respectively. Title pages will be prepared in manuscript.

(Erase heading not required.)

Place	Date	Hour	Summary of Events and Information	Remarks and references to Appendices
MAZINGARBE	7th	4.15 pm	A passenger train was observed travelling North at point H.24.B.	
"		4.30 pm	Smoke was observed rising from LOOS evidently a fire caused by our 4.5 Hows, a thought to be enemy H.Q. house - lasted 1½ hours.	
"	8th	11.30 pm	A/71 fired at G.22.B.9.7 on a working party reported by infantry.	
"		11.10 am	B/71 report two flares seen in their own lines at G.28.C.9.6 – 2 rounds fired.	
"	9th	4.25 pm	A/71 fired on G.22.b.3.0 at report of infantry	
"		11.30 am	B/71 fired on G.28.d.9.5 in retaliation	
"		4.30 pm	A/71 fired on G.28.b.30 + G.22.d.80. in verification (28 rounds).	
"	10th	—	NIL	
"	11th	11 am	Enemy observation balloon appeared to have broken loose – drifted 3° 1km. Disappeared below skyline.	
"		4 pm	B/71 fired 36 rounds on hostile trench in X,1 in retaliation.	
"	12th	1.15 am	A/71 fired 7 rounds on enemy working party on their front line trench in G.28.b. at the request of the infantry.	
"		11.30 am	B/73 fired into LOOS in retaliation G at 1.35 pm. Also reported G.28.d.; G.28.b.; G.23.a.4c.	
"		3.20 pm	A/71 supported G.23.C.6.7, G.23.a.4.2.	
"		5.0 pm	B/71 supported G.28.b.4.0. G.28.b.27, G.28.b.45.	
"		5.30 pm	D/71 fired 28 rounds into enemy front line trenches in X,1 in retaliation –	

WAR DIARY
INTELLIGENCE SUMMARY

Army Form C. 2118

Place	Date	Hour	Summary of Events and Information	Remarks and references to Appendices
MAZINGARBE	Aug '15 13th	2.30pm	A/71 fired on enemy front line trenches in X.2 gave to distract attention from wire cutting operations	Wire cutting operations
"	"	3. pm	B/71 (Same as A/71) and retaliated on X.1 at 6.25.pm.	
"	"	3.pm	C/71 - One fire came up into wire cutting position & repulsed the wire in G.28.6.	
"	"	5. pm	B/71 registered G.22.d.50 and G.23.d.82.	
"	"	6.45 pm	B/73 fired lyddite into LOOS in retaliation.	
"	14th	4.5 pm	A/71 fired at enemy working party in G.23.a.95.	
"	"	7.50 pm	B/71 fired on enemy front line trenches in X.1, in retaliation and
"	15th	5.15 am	A/71 fired on G.28.b.4.5. - B/71 fired on front line trenches in X.1, and on G.28.d.32 and G.28.C.9.1. in retaliation (51 rounds) - D/71 fired
"	"	7.30 am	on enemy front line trenches in G.28.6 in retaliation. B/73 fired lyddite into LOOS in retaliation.
"	"	"	LOOS in retaliation.
"	"	8.5 am	B/71 fired 30 rounds on front trenches in X.1. On G.28.C.9.1 and G.34.C.7.7. in retaliation.	
"	"	8.20 am	B/73 fires lyddite into LOOS in retaliation.	
"	"	10.30 am	A/71 fired on a working party at G.23.a.61. and on G.22.a.82. at 7.pm replying.	
"	"	5.15 pm	B/71 registered enemy front line trench in G.28.b. & up to G.22.d.8.3.	
"	16th	12.20 am	A/71 fires on trenches in G.23.a at report of infantry.	

WAR DIARY

INTELLIGENCE SUMMARY.

(Erase heading not required.)

Army Form C. 2118

Instructions regarding War Diaries and Intelligence Summaries are contained in F. S. Regs., Part II. and the Staff Manual respectively. Title pages will be prepared in manuscript.

Place	Date	Hour	Summary of Events and Information	Remarks and references to Appendices
MAZINGARBE.	Aut.			
	16th	10.40am	A/71 fired on front line trenches in X2 in retaliation, & at G.23.a.41 at 12.10 a.m.	
"	"	11.40am	B/71 registered enemy front line in X2, opposite bryan G.9.A & 9.B. also at 4.30 & 6.20pm	
"	"	12.50am	B/71 fired on enemy front line in X1 in retaliation. A/71 fired on G.22.6.97 in retaliation.	
		till		
"	"	1.15 pm	B/73 fired lyddite into suspected O.P. (house) in LOOS – O.P at G.36.a.58 & on DONBLE CRASSIER.	
"	"	3.10 pm	B/73 fired lyddite into LOOS in retaliation.	
"	17th	11.50am	A/71 fired for the purpose of registering new Zero line. B/71 fired on trenches in retaliation at 3pm	
"	"	5.30 pm	B/71 fired on enemy front line in X1, in retaliation. B/71 fired on G.26 and	
"	"	"	G.28.6.4.5 in retaliation. B/73 retaliated on enemy trenches in G.28.6.	
"	"	12 mn	Completed Registered A/71 who took over O'Klip with 1 Bronze in NOEUX in Reserve.	
"	18th	2.8. am	B/71 fired on G.28.C.6.1 at request of Infantry.	
"	"	8.30 am	B/71 fired on front line trenches in X1 at request of Infantry.	
"	"	2.50 pm	B/71 fired on front line trenches in G.28.6 in retaliation	
"	"	4.30pm	B/71 fired verifying registration. B/71 fired at mortar bombs in G.28.6.27.	
"	"	5.15pm	B/73 fired lyddite into house at G.28.d.0.3 & trenches in G.34.a.7.0 in retaliation.	
"	19th	2.30pm	B/71 fired at working party in trenches in G.28.8. C/71 sprinkled G.22.d.8.3 at 4 pm	
"	"	7.30pm	B/71 fired on front line trenches in X1 in retaliation. B/73 fired lyddite in LOOS in retaliation.	

WAR DIARY
INTELLIGENCE SUMMARY

Army Form C. 2118

Place	Date	Hour	Summary of Events and Information	Remarks and references to Appendices
MAZINGARBE	Aug. 20th	1.15 am	B/71 fired on support trenches in x.1 in retaliation. C/71 fired in G.22.d. at 4 am at enemy working party	
"	"	12 noon	B/73 fired on enemy mortars at G.28.d.36. — and also mortars in G.30.a.80 & G.28.C.5.0. at 6 pm at enemy of infantry	
"	"	4.0 pm	B/71 fired on front line trenches in x,1, also at 5.40 pm & 6.25 pm — all in retaliation.	
"	"	5.0 pm	B/71 fired at reported trench mortars at G.28.b.29. and G.28.B.2.6. in retaliation (24 rounds)	
"	21st	2.15 am	B/71 fires on G.34.b.77 at enemy of infantry	
"	"	9.30 am	C/71 registered G.23.C.37 and G.23.a.85.	Batteries Retaliated when required
"	"	6 pm	B/73 fired at G.29.c.83 with aeroplane observation. Second unreadable at G.29.c.83	
"	22nd	—	Batteries retaliated when required.	
"	23rd	5 pm	B/73 fires with aeroplane observation at G.29.C.8.3. — had light —	
"	"	—	Batteries retaliated when required. B/73 silenced mortar at G.34.a.9.6. at 7 pm	
"	24th	—	Batteries retaliated when required. B/73 silenced mortar in G.28.d. at 9.15 pm	
"	25th	—	Batteries retaliated when required.	
"	26th	—	Nil. Infantry reliefs in progress.	
"	27th	—	Batteries retaliated when required. B/71 registered G.28.6.2 with aeroplane observation.	
"	28th	—	" "	
"	29th	—	B/73 registered known opposite Sap 18. 4 pm	
"	"	—	A/71 relieved B/71 at midnight.	

121/7050

15th Division

B/71 Battery R.F.A.

Vol 2

Aug & Sept. 15.

Army Form C. 2118.

"B" Battery 71st Bde R.F.A.

WAR DIARY
or
INTELLIGENCE SUMMARY.

(Erase heading not required.)

Place	Date	Hour	Summary of Events and Information	Remarks and references to Appendices
PHILOSPHE	27.8.15		RELIEVED BY "A" Battery, 71st Bde R.F.A.	
VAUDRICOURT	27.8.15		REST	
VERMELLES	5.9.15		Took up new position 800 yards N of VERMELLES STN. 150 yards W of VERMELLES STN. LOOS railway line.	
VERMELLES	21.9.15		Commenced wire cutting on the LOOS ROAD REDOUBT	
" "	24.9.15		Wire cutting completed	
" "	25.9.15		Bombardment of German lines	
" "	25.9.15		Battery advanced 500 yards N of FOSSE 7 (QUALITY STREET)	
" "	26.9.15		1 Man (Gnr Hunt A.E.) slightly wounded	

Berkeley Major
Comdg 10/71st Bde R.F.A.

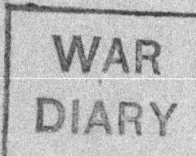

Headquarters,

71st BRIGADE, R.F.A.

(15th Division)

S E P T E M B E R

(29.8.15 to 30.9.15)

1 9 1 5

INTELLIGENCE SUMMARY.

(Erase heading not required.)

Summaries are contained in F. S. Regs., Part II. and the Staff Manual respectively. Title pages will be prepared in manuscript.

Place	Date	Hour	Summary of Events and Information	Remarks and references to Appendices
MAZINGARBE	Aug 29th	—	Batteries retaliated when required.	
"	30th	—	" " " "	
"	31st	—	" " " "	
"	Sept 1st	—	" " " "	
"	2nd	—	" " " "	
"	3rd	—	" " " "	
"	4th	—	" " " "	
"	5th	—	" " " "	
"		—	The right of 5th & 6th B/71 came into their new emplacements from Noeux;	
"		—	And the section of A.C. & D batteries came into their.	
"	6th	—	Batteries retaliated when required, and registered from new positions.	
"		—	On night 6th/7th the remaining sections came up into their new emplacements.	
"	7th	—	Batteries registered new zones.	
"	8th/9th	—	Batteries retaliated when required.	
"	10th	—	" " " " — Direct hit on one 9/1 from 2 heads swooned.	
"	11th/12th	—	Batteries retaliated when required. Registered front line system; and also	
"	20th	—	Cleared line, LOOS and hill 70 with aeroplane observation. (21 targets)	

INTELLIGENCE SUMMARY.

(Erase heading not required.)

Place	Date	Hour	Summary of Events and Information	Remarks and references to Appendices
	SEPT			
PHILOSOPHE	19th	5.0 pm	Brigade headquarters moved into advanced headquarters in PHILOSOPHE.	
"	20th	—	Batteries retaliated when required.	
"	21st to 24th	Day & Night	Preliminary bombardment and wire cutting on SOUTHERN SAP and NORTHERN SALIENT as far as G.28.b.31. Batteries fired on specified areas at night. Infantry patrols inspected the wire each night — reported that it was satisfactorily cut and that the enemy were not repairing it. Saw men digging trenches.	
"	25th	5.50 am	Bombardment by all batteries forming barrages in front of our advancing infantry until 7.5 am. The O.C. brigade went forward to be in communication with G.O.C. 46th Inf. Bde.	
"	"	3.0 pm	D/71 and P/71 advanced to covered position in G.27.b. to support attack on HILL 70.	
"	"	7.30 pm	Brigade headquarters advanced to QUALITY STREET and LOOS ROAD KEEP.	
LOOS ROAD KEEP	26th	2.0 am	A/71 and C/71A to positions in G.29.c and G.34.b.4.6 just west of LOOS in close support of our infantry on the western slopes of HILL 70. These batteries were heavily shelled all day.	
"	"	7.0 pm	A/71 and C/71 came into a position in G.28.b. Brigade headquarters moved to QUALITY STREET. Casualties 1 killed, 2 missing, 11 wounded, and 2 suffering from gas poisoning.	
QUALITY STREET	27th	3.0 pm	All batteries put up a barrage fire on the left flank of the infantry attempt on HILL 70, PUITS 14 BIS, and CHALK PIT WOOD.	
"	"	Night	Barrage fire to the EAST of the LENS – HULLUCH ROAD.	

INTELLIGENCE SUMMARY.
(Erase heading not required.)

Summaries are contained in F. S. Regs., Part II. and the Staff Manual respectively. Title pages will be prepared in manuscript.

Place	Date	Hour	Summary of Events and Information	Remarks and references to Appendices
QUALITY STREET	Sept 28th	—	No found. day or night. Batteries were shelled intermittently, mostly from direction of HULLUCH.	
"	29th	—	" " "	
"	30th	—	" " "	

Howarth Lt Col
7th Bde R.F.A. War Diary up till
the 30th September 1915.

7th Oct. 15

N Hoath Lt Col
Comdg 7, Bde R.F.A.

121/7592.

15th Khroum

71st Bde: R.F.A.
Vol 2

Oct 15

K

CONFIDENTIAL.

71st BRIGADE R.F.A.
WAR DIARY
INTELLIGENCE SUMMARY.
(Erase heading not required.)

Army Form C. 2118.

Instructions regarding War Diaries and Intelligence Summaries are contained in F. S. Regs., Part II. and the Staff Manual respectively. Title pages will be prepared in manuscript.

Place	Date	Hour	Summary of Events and Information	Remarks and references to Appendices
	October			
QUALITY STREET	1st	—	No firing.	
	2nd	—	A/71 & C/71 shelled in the afternoon. Four men wounded.	
	3rd	—	Bde Headquarters moved to de Sauchoy Chateau. Magnificent.	
MAZINGARBE	4th	—	Batteries shelled in morning and afternoon.	
	5th	—	" " " (no damage).	
	6th	—	" " 2 Two Casualties (wounded).	
			Brigade attached to 3rd Infantry Brigade, whose headquarters are at LOOS. Batteries retaliate when required.	
	7th	—	Batteries retaliated when required.	
	8th	—	German counter attack from DOUBLE CRASSIER to HOHENZOLLERN REDOUBT preceded by very heavy bombardment from 12 noon. Batteries retaliated and put up a barrage all along 3rd Infantry Brigade front. Counter attack repulsed all along the line. Artillery fire very effective. A/71 turned onto enemy massed in PUITS 14 Bis to the West Street. Batteries kept up barrage all night. Few Casualties (wounded).	
	9th	—	Batteries retaliated when required and searched enemy trenches and roads in their zones at intervals.	

Army Form C. 2118.

WAR DIARY
INTELLIGENCE SUMMARY.
(Erase heading not required.)

Instructions regarding War Diaries and Intelligence Summaries are contained in F. S. Regs., Part II. and the Staff Manual respectively. Title pages will be prepared in manuscript.

Place	Date	Hour	Summary of Events and Information	Remarks and references to Appendices
MAZINGARBE.	Octob'r 10th	—	Battery commenced wire cutting on trenches South of HULLUCH in the afternoon at 4000 Yds	
"	11th	—	Battery continued wirecutting; an batteries were heavily shelled — A/71 had a direct hit on a dug out — 5 killed and 3 wounded.	
"	12th	—	Batteries continued wirecutting. A/71 battery heavily shelled all day.	
"	13th	—	A/71 had 11 casualties including their B.S.M. also one casualty in B/71. B/71 & D/71 continued wirecutting until 11 a.m. an batteries began bombardment of enemy trenches South of HULLUCH at 1 p.m; and supported their infantry (1st Bde) assault at 2.0 p.m.	
"	14th	—	Batteries retaliated when required.	
"	15th	—	" " " "	
"	16th	—	new battery positions in VERMELLES relieving 1st Division at 8.0 p.m. One section for battery moved into Battery registered new zone (in front of HULLUCH). Two wounded.	
"	17th	6 a.m	Remaining section of battery came into VERMELLES POSITIONS, in support of Left battalion of 47th Division in front of HULLUCH.	
"	18th	"	Battery retaliated when required.	

Army Form C. 2118.

WAR DIARY
or
INTELLIGENCE SUMMARY

(Erase heading not required.)

Instructions regarding War Diaries and Intelligence Summaries are contained in F.S. Regs., Part II. and the Staff Manual respectively. Title pages will be prepared in manuscript.

Place	Date	Hour	Summary of Events and Information	Remarks and references to Appendices
MAZINGARBE	Oct. 19th	—	Batteries retaliated when required — and registered new zone in front of CITÉ ST ÉLIE to N. of HULLUCH to be taken over next day.	
"	20th	7.am	The 71st Brigade R.F.A. took over the new zone (see above) supporting the 15th Division. Both Batteries continued registering and retaliated when required.	
"	"	—		
"	21st	—	Batteries continued registering and retaliated when necessary.	
"	till	—	" " " "	
"	28th	—	" " " "	
"	29th	—	Batteries retaliated when required. Frightfulness on ST ÉLIE at 3.a.m. and 5.a.m. [2 drivers C/71, one S.S.4 one driver B/71, wounded — 11 horses killed]	
"	30th	—	Batteries retaliated when required. [One horse killed in A/71]	
"	31st	—	" " " Frightfulness on enemy trenches between HULLUCH and ST ÉLIE at 1.0.am.	

1/11/15.

J.W.Heath Lt. Col.
Commanding 71st Bde R.F.A.

15th Division G.1116/

Special Divisional Order.

The following message has been received from Sir Henry Rawlinson:-

"The Corps Commander is anxious that you should communicate to all ranks of the 15th Division his high appreciation of the admirable fighting spirit which they displayed in the attack & capture of LOOS village & HILL 70.

Sir Douglas Haig has also desired the Corps Commander to convey his congratulations to the Division."

The Major General wishes writes to say that he is very proud of his Command.

Sd. J Burnett Stuart
Lt. Col.
General Staff.

27 Sept 15.

Special Order

Issued with 15th Divisional Routine Orders of 16.10.15.

The Brigadier General Commanding 15th Divisional Artillery wishes to place on record the Excellent work performed by the 71st Brigade R.F.A. in action during the period September 25th to October 14th under most difficult and trying circumstances.

He wishes to convey his thanks to all ranks for their steady & gallant conduct.

sd J.H. Sherbrooke, Major.
Brigade Major 15th D.A.

71 H Bde. BHQ.
vol 3

14/7936

15th K.H.

WAR DIARY

INTELLIGENCE SUMMARY.

71st Brigade R.F.A.

Army Form C. 2118.

Place	Date 1915 Nov:	Hour	Summary of Events and Information	Remarks and references to Appendices
VERMELLES.	1st to 6th	—	Batteries retaliated when required.	
"	7th	—	" " "	
"	8th	—	" " " We had a NIGHT FRIGHTFULNESS.	
"	10th	—	" " " We had a midday FRIGHTFULNESS.	
"	15th	—	" " " Sections of each battery were relieved	
"	"	—	by the 70th Bde R.F.A.; and went back to NOEUX-LES-MINES.	
"	16th	—	Batteries retaliated when required and 70th Bde sections registered.	
"	"	—	Last sections were relieved by 70th Bde at 8.0 p.m. The first sections	
"	"	—	went back to GOSNAY, the last went to NOEUX. Bryde H.Q. moved to GOSNAY.	
"	17th	—	Second sections moved back to join the rest of the batteries in billets	
"	"	—	in GOSNAY. B.A.C. remained at VERQUIN.	
GOSNAY.	18th to 21st	—	In rest billets.	
"	22nd	—	A section from each battery moved up and relieved sections of 12th B.A.	
"	—	—	in action in ANNEQUIN (TOURBIÈRES LOOP) by 5.0 p.m.	
"	—	—	2nd Division in action in our left (41st Bde R.F.A.) - 70th Bde in VERMELLES on our right.	

Army Form C. 2118.

71st Bde R.F.A.

WAR DIARY
INTELLIGENCE SUMMARY.
(Erase heading not required.)

Instructions regarding War Diaries and Intelligence Summaries are contained in F. S. Regs., Part II. and the Staff Manual respectively. Title pages will be prepared in manuscript.

Place	Date 1915	Hour	Summary of Events and Information	Remarks and references to Appendices
	Nov.			
ANNEQUIN	23rd	—	The second sections came up from GOSNAY and the brigade took over the new bit of the line (HOHENZOLLERN REDOUBT) from the 12th D.A. by 5.0 p.m.	
"	24th to 30th	—	The first sections registered their new zones. Shagun huts in SAILLY + VERQUINEUL. S.O.H.Q. as before at VERQUIN. Batteries continued registering thir zones. The enemy fairly quiet; we had several threatened FRIGHTFULNESS to which he didn't retaliate very much.	

M W Wratth Lt. Colonel.
Com. dg 71st Bde R.F.A.

71st Batt: RFA.
Vol: 4

131/7910

15th Nov

CONFIDENTIAL.

71st Bde. R.F.A. WAR DIARY

INTELLIGENCE SUMMARY.

Army Form C. 2118.

Place	Date 1915	Hour	Summary of Events and Information	Remarks and references to Appendices
ANNEQUIN	Dec. 1st to 14th	—	Batteries retaliated when required. He had several divisional FRIGHTFULNESS on ST ELIE, HOHENZOLLERN and HAISNES.	
"	15th	—	Batteries retaliated when required. One section of each battery was relieved by sections of the 6th London R.F.A. at 5.0 p.m.	
"	16th	—	Batteries retaliated when required and new sections registered them the defence of zones. The second sections were relieved by 6.0 p.m. and a portion of the line handed over to O.C. 6th London R.F.A.	
"	—	—	The brigade marched back to AUCHEL into rest billets, by batteries and were all in billets by 9.0 p.m.	
"	—	—	In Rest billets in AUCHEL. D.A. Headquarters at MARLES LES MINES and the 70th Bde. The 71st Bde R.F.A. 9 less one battery 73rd Bde. still up in action under 47th Division, who took over our divisional frontage.	
AUCHEL	14th to 31st	—		

J W Heath Lt Col
Com- dg 71st Bde R.F.A.

3rd Jan '16

CONFIDENTIAL.

JANUARY 1916.

91st Brigade R.F.A.

Army Form C. 2118.

WAR DIARY
or
INTELLIGENCE SUMMARY.
(Erase heading not required.)

Instructions regarding War Diaries and Intelligence Summaries are contained in F. S. Regs., Part II. and the Staff Manual respectively. Title pages will be prepared in manuscript.

Place	Date	Hour	Summary of Events and Information	Remarks and references to Appendices
AUCHEL	1916			
	Jan 1st to 3rd		In billets at AUCHEL (in 4th Corps reserve)	
	4th	11.15	Major Berkley 8/th Promoted Lieut Colonel & ordered 91st Brigade R.F.A.	
	5th	9.0 am	Started on Divisional Route March. 91st Brigade R.F.A. formed part of the Advanced Guard.	
		3.0 pm	Halt orders received. Base Wagons, & A & D Batteries billeted in BEAUMETZ LEZ AIRE. B & C billeted in KNOR.	
	6th	9.30 am	91st Brigade marched to DONNE BROEUCQ and selected positions in which to come into action.	
		12 noon	Operations abandoned owing to thick mist & rain & all units returned to same billets as occupied on night 5/6th Jany.	
	7th to 12th			
	13th		Marched back to AUCHEL.	
	14th		Captain C.F.P. Mackenzie 11th Battery posted to command B Battery.	
	15th		In billets at AUCHEL.	
	16th		Bne Neelson and Bailey went into action in FOSSE 4 and relieving batteries of 91st Division as follows:-	

WAR DIARY

INTELLIGENCE SUMMARY

71st Brigade R.F.A.   Army Form C. 2118.

Place	Date	Hour	Summary of Events and Information	Remarks and references to Appendices
AUCHEL	16"		1 Section from A Battery relieved 1 Section 46" Battery R.F.A. (Capt. Ridgeway) at G.26d.7.7	(Sheet 36C N⁰ 43 Ed 6)
			1 " " B " " 1 " 46" "	
			1 " " C " " 1 " 51" " (Major White) G.27c.1.2	
			1 " " D " " 1 " 114" " (Major Fairbairn) G.33a.8.5	
			The above sections carried out registration of points in their zones during the day. Remaining Sections of each Battery - Brigade Headquarters and Brigade moved up into action.	
			Bde Hqrs taking over from 39" Bde R.F.A. (Lt Col he Naughton) in Boulevard Magingarbe at L.23.d.1½.9	
			Bde A.C. from Sp⁰ Bde A.C. in VERQUIN	
			Took over 1461 rounds Shrapnel. 1183 rounds High Explosive from 1"Div Batteries.	
			Ammunition Expended 290.	
MAZINGARBE	17"		A & B Btys are digging new Gun pits + dugouts & so fire very little.	
			B Bty moved their guns to position at G.26.d.4.2 where they are digging a fresh position.	

WAR DIARY
INTELLIGENCE SUMMARY

Army Form C. 2118.

7/Y Brigade RFA

Place	Date	Hour	Summary of Events and Information	Remarks and references to Appendices
MAZINGARBE	18th		Enemy shelled 65 RetzePoint, LOOS & front line in H.31.c. with 4.2's v/aphs from direction of CITE ST AUGUSTE. C & D Batys continued registering – A.T.B. still digging. Amn. Exp. 74.	
	19th	11.30am	Enemy shelled MAZINGARBE for 20 minutes. Guns Exp. 32	
	20th		8/1st Guns in their new pits. Amn Exp. 279. Enemy fired at enemy working parties & an installation. B/1st had 4 direct hits on house at H.31. Q.29 Reported to be a M.G. Amn Exp. 104.	
	21st			
	22nd		Germans seen working in their trenches at H.31.d central – they were dispersed by 13 rounds shrapnel from A/71. Amn Exp. 10.0.	
	23rd		Germans very busy working on their trenches also on their wire on 2nd line. They were dispersed by our shrapnel fire each time.	
	23/24	12.45am	"Test Attack" deemed from 13th Div. Our East Battery fired 30 rounds after interval from B.Q. per Lieut on its bright lights. 1st round fired 30 seconds after interval from B.Q. last round fired 2 minutes after.	

Army Form C. 2118.

W? Brigade RFA

WAR DIARY
or
INTELLIGENCE SUMMARY.
(Erase heading not required.)

Instructions regarding War Diaries and Intelligence Summaries are contained in F. S. Regs., Part II. and the Staff Manual respectively. Title pages will be prepared in manuscript.

Place	Date	Hour	Summary of Events and Information	Remarks and references to Appendices
MAZINGARBE	23rd		Amn Exp. 23.	
	24th		A/B registering all points in their own zone. Amn Exp. 200.	
	25th		A/71 knocked out a M.G. emplacement & a Lt Lieutenant at H.31.c.P.? German Artillery very active on trenches in Brigade zone. 100s - 200s exhausted	
			Q QUALITY STREET. Amn Exp. 209.	
			No. Y/815/3 Gunner Bruce B/71 Killed in action	
			41207 " HAIGH B/71 Wounded " Eat died in Field Amb NOEUX X.	
	26th		German artillery very active. Loos & Fosse 8 Shelled all day. Amn Exp. 302.	
	27th		Batteries retaliated on CITE ST AUGUSTE & enemies Batteries in that place. Hostile front was very heavily shelled by enemy all day. Retaliation by 18pr Btys seemed to have little effect. Amn Exp. 650.	
	28th		German artillery very active along whole of Brigade front, on 008, 6 Shelepone and FOSSE Y.	

Army Form C. 2118.

11th Brigade RFA

WAR DIARY
or
INTELLIGENCE SUMMARY.
(Erase heading not required.)

Place	Date	Hour	Summary of Events and Information	Remarks and references to Appendices
MAZINGARBE	28th	1.0 p.m	Enemy bombarded CHALK PIT WOOD very heavily until 2.15pm when they lifted & formed a barrage about 150-200 yds west of it for about 20 minutes. No infantry action followed. After this enemy shelling practically ceased. 18p. detonation again had little effect. Amm. Exp. 486.	
	29th		Enemy shelled our front trenches in Bay 3 x 1005 intermittently B/71 retaliated on CITE ST AUGUSTE & silencing fire coming from that direction. Amm. Exp. 840. Ro. 9525. Gunner C.S. WALTERS killed in action C/71. Batteries carried out 3 shoots/schemes as ordered by D.A. Otherwise enemy artillery quiet.	A
	30th		Roos shelled from midday to 2.0 pm observation impossible owing to light in afternoon. Amm. Exp. 720.	
	31st		Enemy made 6 new saps in Bay zone. 150 rounds was fired at these during the night by A/71 to prevent work being done on them. This fire was reported to be very effective by 2Lt Thompson who was in the front trench during the night. Normal rate of fire on strength of Brigade etc attached	B

W Rothenberger
Lieut W.11 Brigade

CONFIDENTIAL. FEBRUARY 1916.

71st BRIGADE R7A Army Form C. 2118.

WAR DIARY

INTELLIGENCE SUMMARY.

(Erase heading not required.)

Instructions regarding War Diaries and Intelligence Summaries are contained in F. S. Regs., Part II. and the Staff Manual respectively. Title pages will be prepared in manuscript.

Place	Date	Hour	Summary of Events and Information	Remarks and references to Appendices
MAZINGARBE	Feb 1st		Enemy shelled Front & Support Trenches KLOOS intermittently to which we retaliated. Ann. Exp. 698.	
	2nd		All new Saps were registered. Retaliation & enemy shelling 1008 Trenches. Ann. Exp. 179.	
	3rd		Registration continued. Ann. Exp. 90.	
	4th		Enemy shelled QUALITY STREET with 5.9's from direction of BENIFONTAINE. C/71 stopped rows running E+W about H.26.c.60 from 12.15am to 5.45am at irregular intervals. Ann. Exp. 1100.	
	5th		From 10.0am to 1.30pm an enemy H. Battery shelled 9/71 at 3 min intervals. One direct hit on Telephone dugout - no damage done & no casualties to 9/71. No 1379 Pt. Anning E. C/71 } wounded in action. 81580 Pt. Queen J.S. C/71 } Ann. Exp. 24.4.	
	6th		C/71 reported flashes from enemy battery in front of WINGLES WATER TOWER. 8" Hows turned on & got a direct hit on to one of Hows where the flashes appeared to come from. Ann. Exp. 252	

WAR DIARY
INTELLIGENCE SUMMARY

1/3 Brigade R.F.A.

Army Form C. 2118.

Place	Date	Hour	Summary of Events and Information	Remarks and references to Appendices
MAZINGARBE	7th		C/71 Attempted to streak hits with HE on a suspected enemy Company HQ in trenches at H32a53. Amm. Exp. 265.	
	8th		Fosse 7 shelled from 12.30pm to 1.30 pm with about 100 shells, good proportion being lachrymatory shells. No damage. Amm. Exp. 428.	
	9th		Quiet day. Amm. Exp. J 121.	
	10th		D/71 observed a German in the water tower at FEMME DES MINES.	
	11th		DE LENS. Amm. Exp. 293. Enemy shelled LOOS & trenches in Du Bois intermittently. Retaliation on BOIS DE QUATORZE stopped this. Amm. Exp. 220.	
	12th		C/71 knocked in a MG emplacement at H31 d22.5 + the bench opposite. Both scores. Amm. Exp. 222.	
	13th		Gun was seen in Sap E9-14. C/71 fired at same but very close. Amm. Exp. 290.	
	14th		Quiet day. Amm. Exp. 120.	
	15th		Quiet day — 163.	
	16th		Big enemy working party lower J points 20 & 11 chains at M11 A14 blown down. Amm. Exp. 153.	

WAR DIARY / INTELLIGENCE SUMMARY

Army Form C. 2118. 7th Brigade BHQ

Place	Date	Hour	Summary of Events and Information	Remarks and references to Appendices
MAZINGARBE	17th		B/71 remounted M.G. loopholes at H25 c96 r43 c16. Quiet day. Amm Exp 153	
	18th		Quiet day. Amm Exp 163.	
	19th		A grant barrage was seen about N1 & 99 i arranged by B/71 it was soon taken down. Amm Exp 201	
			15th German Anti Aircraft Shells failed to burst in the air &	
	20th		dropped by a/m bursting on percussion. Amm Exp. 150	
			Lose Y Heavily shelled heavily from 2-6 pm. Amm Exp. 149	
	21st		Quiet day. 20S Amm Exp.	
(to 22nd)			No 22189 B. Armit G. B/71 wounded in action	
21st			Quiet throughout day. Amm Exp. 355	
23rd	9.30pm		Enemy shelled road on southern edge of FOSSE 7, & caught a	
			wagon of B/71.	
			Lieut B J Geere B/71 killed	
			2nd Lt. Thompson B/71 wounded No. 16183 Sr. Slater B/71 wounded	
			Lieut Sr Miller TB. B/71 "	
			No. 9166 Sr. Lawson B/71 killed 73365 Sr. Revernes B/71 "	
			24374 Sr. Peterson B/71 "	
			19118 Sr. Page B/71 "	

WAR DIARY
or
INTELLIGENCE SUMMARY

Army Form C. 2118.

4th Bn RDF

Place	Date	Hour	Summary of Events and Information	Remarks and references to Appendices
MAZINGARBE	24th	—	Quiet day. A few H.E's on FOSSE 7 area. Annm Exp. 82. Lieut K.R.F. Dennistoun attached 8/71 Slightly wounded. Br. 11727 Br. Moore F.F. 8/71	
	25th		Quiet day. Annm Exp. 20	
	26th	8.30am 10am	8/71 fired at German working parties with good effect - Shortly afterwards were heard in German trench. Annm Exp. 109	
	27th		8/71 fired at Enemy O.P. at H.32.c.14 & got one direct hit. This seemed to annoy Hun observer who immediately fired as this O.P. of our Divisional Intelligence Officer. Annm Exp. 300	
	28th		8/71 killed a German sentry in their trench about H.31.a.6. Annm Exp. 238.	
	29th		Quiet day. Annm Exp. 31st.	

JWHeath
Lt Col RA
Comdg 4th Bde RHA

Army Form C. 2118.

4th Brigade R.F.A

WAR DIARY
INTELLIGENCE SUMMARY.
(Erase heading not required.)

Place	Date	Hour	Summary of Events and Information	Remarks and references to Appendices
MAZINGARBE	MARCH 1st		80.9489 Bdr TWITCHITT 6/71 wounded 29/2/16. 82952 S. SPENCE 6/71 " "	
	2nd		During night — Ann Exp. 158.	
	3rd		Enemy shelled all round 6/71 Bty position from 10:30 am 5 rounds light 5" 9's. Quiet day — Ann Exp. 80.	
	4th		— D/71. Silenced enemy positions on H31c. Ann Exp. 104	
			Enemy shelled B/71 and C/71 Bty positions between 6.0 am and 7.30 am with 5.9's & 4.2 hows.	
	5th		D/71 knocked out M.G. emplacement at H31 L.1.4. Ann Exp. 173.	
	6th		Objs. registered points by aeroplane. Ann Exp. 63	
			Numerous men working parties dispersed. Enemy trench mortars stoffed. Several aerial hits. Ann Exp. 120.	
	7th		Quiet day. Ann Exp. 235.	
	8th		Enemy fairly active shelling our front support & communication trenches. Ann Exp. 86.	
	9th		C/71 staged Hostile O.P's at H32.c.16.2 & H31.d.43.4 with success also H31.d.37 where a log had been put up. Ann Exp. 217.	

WAR DIARY
INTELLIGENCE SUMMARY.

Army Form C. 2118.

1/4 Brigade RGA

Place	Date	Hour	Summary of Events and Information	Remarks and references to Appendices
MAZINGARBE	10/16	-	Enemy shelled our trenches & cross trenches we retaliated. Amm Exp.	222
	11/16		Enemy trench mortars active. These were silenced by our fire. Amm Exp.	121
	12/16		Enemy Battery apparently in BOIS DE QUATORZE was very active on our trenches. B/11 staged a M.G.emplacement H.31.C.1.8.3. - 17 direct hits	777
			Amm. Exp. 171. L. 69267 Lecorles MASON C/11 wounded in NOEUX LES MINES by fragment of a bomb.	
	13/16		Quiet day - Amm. Exp. 195- No. 9491 L. MILLMAN C/11 wounded	
	14/16		20586V area shelled very heavily from 7.0am to 12.30 pm also 5.9s & 2/20cm the direction of LENS. C/11 had 18 direct hits on Pumpits & dugouts. no damage to material. C/11 had to 4 gun completely knocked out.	
			No 627 Arm Artificer FRANCIS (Bde HQ.) wounded	
			82423 Cpl GRAY A/11 wounded afterwards died of wounds.	
			Capt Alan Patterson (Comdg D/11) killed in action by a fragment of H.2. shell.	
			Amm Exp. 60	
	15/16		A Quiet day. Ammunition Exp. 65.	
	16/16		Quiet day. Blg's destroyed found by aeroplane. Amm Exp. 83	
	17/16		Much movement observed along trench from H.32.a.7.2 to C.8.9.2. Amm Exp.	38

WAR DIARY

INTELLIGENCE SUMMARY.

(Erase heading not required.)

Army Form C. 2118.

1/4th Bn R.D.F.

Place	Date	Hour	Summary of Events and Information	Remarks and references to Appendices
MAZINGARBE	18th		Enemies new working parties dispersed by our fire. Ann. Exp. 94	
	19th		Quiet day. Ann. Exp. 95	
	20th		Quiet day. Ann. Exp. 92. Beacon from 6/180 "that 16th Div. attacked"	
	21st		To a/n for instruction	
			Quiet day Ann. Exp 64	
	22nd		—do— 84	
	23rd		—do— 71	
	24th		—do— 63	
	25th		—do— 26.	
	26th		Enemy working parties very active – dispersed by our fire. Ann. Exp. 69	
	27th		Working parties again active. Ann. Exp. 27	
	28th		Quiet day. Ann. Exp. 28	
	29th		—do— 61	
	30th		—do— 34	
	31st		—do— 86.	

J.W. Rath(?) Lt Colonel
Commdg 1/4 Bn R.D.Fus(?)

1-4-16.

WAR DIARY or INTELLIGENCE SUMMARY

Army Form C. 2118.

71st Brigade RFA

Place	Date	Hour	Summary of Events and Information	Remarks and references to Appendices
MAZINGARBE	April 1st		Enemy shelled all round C/71 & D/71 wk 5.9's. Amm. expended 50.	
	2nd		Quiet day at Batteries. LOOS heavily shelled in the morning and cellars which contained telephone exchange was blown in. Amm expended 79. No 1926 Gnr Cracknell J.T. D/71 killed in action. No 9168 Gnr Irwin C/71 wounded.	
	3rd		Quiet day. Carried out some registrations. Amm expended. 25.	
	4th		Several enemy working parties observed and dispersed. Amm expended 43.	
	5th		Enemy fairly active with 4.2's on LOOS. We retaliated with good effect. Amm expended. 49.	
	6th		LOOS and our front system quite heavily shelled all day. We retaliated with good effect. Amm expended 192.	
	7th		Quiet day. Amm expended 78.	
	8th		Quiet day. At about 7 p.m. 1st Divis on our right blew a camouflet. 5 red rockets were observed and our batteries opened a barrage on enemy lines. Amm expended. 79.	
	9th		Numerous working parties observed and strafed. Amm expended. 180.	

71st Brigade RFA
II

Army Form C. 2118.

WAR DIARY
or
INTELLIGENCE SUMMARY.
(Erase heading not required.)

Place	Date	Hour	Summary of Events and Information	Remarks and references to Appendices
MAZINGARBE	10th	-	Vicinity of A/71 heavily shelled with 5.9's persistently all the morning. Nearly all rounds fell short in Crons de Fosse 7. No material or personal damage done. Amm. expended 148.	
	11th	-	Quiet day. Amm. expended 59.	
	12th	-	Two reported enemy O.P.'s blown in. Amm expended 44	
	13th	-	Quiet day. Amm expended 53.	
	14th	-	LOOS and our trenches fairly heavily shelled. We retaliated with good effect. Amm expended 81	
	15th	-	Quiet day. Right section relieved by section of 180th Brigade RFA. 16th Div. and left section go back to AMES leaving guns behind "in situ", personnel going by Motor lorry. Amm expended 22.	
	16th	-	Quiet day. Relief completed. Remaining sections go back to AMES. Amm expended 36.	
AMES	17th	-	Brigade in Rest billets at AMES	
	18th	-		
	19th	-		

Army Form C. 2118.

WAR DIARY
or
INTELLIGENCE SUMMARY.

71st Brigade R.F.A. /11

(Erase heading not required.)

Instructions regarding War Diaries and Intelligence Summaries are contained in F.S. Regs., Part II. and the Staff Manual respectively. Title pages will be prepared in manuscript.

Place	Date	Hour	Summary of Events and Information	Remarks and references to Appendices
AMES	April 20th	—	Brigade in rest billets at AMES.	
	21st	—	—	
	22nd	—	—	
	23rd	—	—	
	24th	—	—	
	25th	—	— Marching order Parade. March past Brig. Gen. McNaughton on taking over command of 15th D.A.	
	26th	—	Gas attack in the LOOS Salient suspected. The 4 Batteries march up to NOEUX-LES-MINES and come under orders of G.O.C. 16th D.A. Batteries get into action after dark, as sections attached to 16th D.A. Batteries. (Making 6 gun Btys)	
	27th	—	Enemy launched a gas attack on LOOS Salient, and took over front trenches but were bombed out by 16th Division.	
	28th	—	Situation fairly quiet again. First sections transfer to ANNEQUIN	
	29th	—	Brigade HQrs. march up to Noyelles and take over from 12th D.A. Left Group. Second Sections transfer to ANNEQUIN	
NOYELLES	30th	—	Quiet day. Batteries in position at ANNEQUIN.	Nicolson [signature] Lt. Col. Comdg 71st Bgde R.F.A

War Diary

Left Group Operation Order No. 1

Copy No. 8

Ref. Sheet 36 c. N.W. 1 & 3 1/10,000
& Sheet 36 B. N.E. 1/20,000

27-4-16.

1. Ref. 15th Divl. Arty Operation Order No 23 dated 25-4-16.

2. Left Group H.Q. will be at L.11.b.5.1.

3. The Frontage of Left Group will be from A.28.c.8.12. to G.5.d.7.4.

   This will be divided between 18 pr. Batteries as follows:

   D/71.   A.28.c.8.12.   to   G.4.b.3.9.
   B/71.   G.4.b.3.9.   to   G.4.b.4.3.
   A/71.   G.4.b.4.3.   to   G.4.d.6.8.
   C/71.   G.4.d.6.8.   to   G.4.d.9.5½.
   C/70.   G.4.d.9.5½.   to   G.5.c.7½.5.
   B/70.   G.5.c.7½.5.   to   G.5.d.

   D/73 & C/73 as a 6 gun How. Bty. will distribute their fire over the whole of the Group Frontage.

4. Batteries will take over night lines points from the Batteries of 12th Division which they are relieving.

5. Batteries will verify registration taken over, by their sections on 29th & 30th inst.

6. O.C. C/71 will detail an officer to report at Right Battalion H.Q. GORDON ALLEY at 3 p.m. on 29th inst.
   & O.C. D/71 an officer to report at Left Battalion H.Q. CANNON STREET at same time & on the same day.

7. O.C. Batteries will report to LEFT Group H.Q. by telephone when their reliefs are completed on 29th inst.

8. Acknowledge.

Nicholson
2nd Lieut. R.F.A.
& Adjutant
Left Group 15th D.A.

Copy No 1   to   A/71
   "   " 2   "   B/71
   "   " 3   "   C/71
   "   " 4   "   D/71
   "   " 5   "   B/70
   "   " 6   "   C/70
   "   " 7   "   D/73
   "   " 8   "   War Diary
   "   " 9   "   File

War Diary

71st Brigade RFA Operation Order No 5

Ref Sheet 36 c N.W.1.3
1/40000
27-4-16

1. Ref 15th Div Arty Operation Order no 23 dated 25/4/16

2. Gun Pits, Guns, Stores &c.
   These will be taken over from Btys of 64th Bde as follows:—

	Gun Pits	Guns Stores &c.
D/71	4 most Northerly Pits	2 from A/64, 2 from D/64
B/71	4 next	2 — A/64, 2 — D/64
A/71	4 next	4 — B/64
C/71	4 most Southerly	4 — C/64

   The two guns of A/64 which will be taken over by B/71 are to be brought from RUITOIRE on night 27th/28th to A/64 wagon line by A/64, and will be taken over by B/71 at this wagon line.

   These guns must be put into their pits on night 28th/29th

3. Wagon Lines
   These will be taken over from Batterys of 64th Bde RFA as follows:—

D/71 from	D/64
B/71 "	A/64
A/71 "	B/64
C/71 "	C/64

4. Zones
   The zone of 71st Bde RFA will be from a 21 c 8.2 to G 4 d 9.3½.
   This will be divided between Btys as follows:—

D/71 A 28 c 8 1/2 to G 4 c 39

B/71 G 4 c 39 to G 4 c 43

A/71 G 4 c 43 to G 4 d 68

C/71 G 4 d 68 to G 4 d 95½

5. Night Lines

Night Line Points will be taken over as far as possible from Btys of 64th Bde RFA

6. Registration

Registration taken over will be verified on 29th & 30th

7. Ref Para 6 15th DA Operation order no 23

Wagon Line Sections will move under Battery arrangements to reach their new Wagon lines at 7.0 pm.

8. Battys will report to Left Group HQ. when reliefs are completed on 29th

9. Acknowledge.

Nicholson
/ Lieut. R.F.A.
Adjutant 71st Brigade R.F.A.

Copy No 1 to A/71
    No 2   B/71
    No 3   C/71
    No 4   D/71
    No 5   BAC/71
    No 6   War Diary
    No 7   File

Army Form C. 2118.

71st Brigade R.F.A.

WAR DIARY
or
INTELLIGENCE SUMMARY.
(Erase heading not required.)

Place	Date	Hour	Summary of Events and Information	Remarks and references to Appendices
NOYELLES.	May 1st	.	Considerable shelling of our trenches to which we retaliated vigorously. Am. expd 109	
"	2nd	.	D/71 silenced an enemy battery. Various registrations carried out. Am. expd. 142.	
"	3.	.	Retaliation for enemy shelling carried out all day. A/71 dispersed a working party. Am. expd. 224.	
"	4.	.	C/71 bombarded enemy's trenches. D/71 again silenced an enemy battery. Am. expd. 197.	
"	5.	.	Our trenches were heavily shelled. We retaliated vigorously. Am. expended 247.	
"	6.	-	Still heavy shelling of our trenches. Our batteries carried out an organised bombardment in retaliation which must have done much damage. Am. expended 656.	
"	7.	.	Large Minenwerfer very active on our trenches. C/71 dispersed a working party. Am. expd. 308.	
"	8.	.	C & D/71 Battery positions shelled with 4.2's & 5.9's. D/71 dispersed a working party & obtained 4 direct hits on a machine gun emplacement. Am. expd. 154.	
"	9.	.	A/71 blew in 3 loopholes. D/71 set a dug-out on fire. B/71 damaged enemy parapet. Amt. expd. 384.	
"	10.	.	Large minenwerfer discovered firing from behind the DUMP. Am. expd. 229.	
"	11.	.	Up to 3.45 p.m. everything was comparatively quiet. At 3.45 p.m. enemy started shelling our front line which increased in violence until at 4.5 it became	

T.1134. Wt. W708—776. 500000. 4/15. Sir J. C. & S.

Army Form C. 2118.

WAR DIARY
or
INTELLIGENCE SUMMARY. 71st Brigade R.F.A.
(Erase heading not required.)

Place	Date	Hour	Summary of Events and Information	Remarks and references to Appendices
NOYELLES	May 12	11"Codn"?	intense. This bombardment consisted chiefly of very heavy minenwerfer on his trenches and 5.9's 4.2's on road junctions and battery positions. At 4.15 his bombardment reached an unprecedented violence and 2 large mines were blown, after which enemy launched an attack. They succeeded in getting a footing in about 500 yards of our trenches to the depth of 300 yds. All batteries kept up barrage all through, well supported counter attacks at 10.pm. D/71 had 2 direct hits on 2 pits but no damage was done to the guns. Both of which were in action within 3 hours. Gas shell were freely used by enemy, but our layers telephonists had their duties in smoke helmets for some 16 hours. Casualties - No 4100. Sergt Sampson A/71 wounded. No 81793. Gnr Surtees J. C/71 wounded. No 82780 Bsr Flanagan R. C/71 wounded. Amn: expended 3582.	
"	13		We continued to bombard enemy trenches, & registered ANCHOR TRENCH which enemy had captured. Amm: expended 1080.	

WAR DIARY
or
INTELLIGENCE SUMMARY. 71st B.ᵈᵉ R.F.A.

(Erase heading not required.)

Army Form C. 2118.

Place	Date	Hour	Summary of Events and Information	Remarks and references to Appendices
NOYELLES.	13ᵗʰ	—	A quiet day. Amm expended 124.	
	14	—	Our batteries were heavily shelled. Casualties. No 40984 Sgt Sullis B.C. A/71 wounded. 2215 Dr Nice J. B.A.C./71 killed. 18366 Gnr Williams G.H. B/71 died of wounds. 75403 Dr Langston W. B.A.C./71 wounded. 68294 Gnr Andrews B.A.C./71 wounded. 59094 Gnr Sibley C. B/71 wounded. 61387 Sergt Preece J.F. C/71 wounded. 83567 Gnr Beard F. C/71 wounded. 103967 Gnr Laws C. C/71 wounded. 7941 Gnr Watts J.A. C/71 wounded. Amm: expended. 1243.	
"	15ᵗʰ	—	A quiet day. Amm: expended 84.	
"	16ᵗʰ	—	C/71 Shelled heavily shelled in morning. No damage or casualties. Amm: exps. 86.	
"	17ᵗʰ	—	We carried out a bombardment on HOHENZOLLERN REDOUBT. Enemy's retaliation was very heavy. Amm: exp. 963.	
"	18ᵗʰ	—	A quiet day. Amm exp. 60.	
"	19ᵗʰ	—	Our batteries retaliated to vigorous fire from heavy Minenwerfer. Amm. exps. 129.	
"	20ᵗʰ	—	A quiet day. Amm. exps. 267.	
"	21ˢᵗ	—	A mine was blown by enemy between HOHENZOLLERN REDOUBT & QUARRIES. We barraged the far lip & prevented enemy from occupying it. Amm. exp. 365.	

Army Form C. 2118.

WAR DIARY
or
INTELLIGENCE SUMMARY. 71st Brigade RFA.
(Erase heading not required.)

Place	Date	Hour	Summary of Events and Information	Remarks and references to Appendices
NOYELLES	22nd	-	A quiet day. Amm. expended. 2 5 7.	
"	23rd	-	Enemy exploded a mine near QUARRIES otherwise a quiet day. Amm. exp. 2 6 9.	
"	24th	-	A quiet day. Amm. expended. 2 5 2.	
"	25th	-	Hostile minenwerfer very active. We blew a mine at 9 p.m. and barrage) communication trenches etc. Enemy retaliated very heavily. Amm. exp. 1 0 5.	
"	26th	-	D/71 engaged suspected O.P. and registered 3 direct hits. A & B/71 engaged loopholes with good result. Amm. exp. 2 6 7.	
"	27th	-	Hostile artillery very active all day. Our batteries kept busy retaliating. Amm. exp. 2 2 4.	
"	28th	-	Hostile field guns + minenwerfer very active.	
"	29th	-	D/71 reinforced by one section from 64th Bde RFA. 12th Divn. Amm exp. 8 2 4.	
"	30th	-	C/71 reinforced by one section from 64th B. RFA. 12th Div. Amm. exp. 2 0 2.	
"	31st	-	A quiet day. Amm expended. 2 0 6.	

J W Strath Lt. Col. RFA
Comdg 71st Bde RFA.

WAR DIARY

Left Group
71st ...... BRIGADE R. F. A.
15th Divisional Artillery

HQ 71 Bde RFA.
A B C & D/71
B & C/70
D/73 & ....
& C/73.

May
1916

Army Form C. 2118.

WAR DIARY
or
INTELLIGENCE SUMMARY.

Left Group 15th D.A. A/71, B/71, C/71, D/71 H.Q. 71
B/70 C/70 D/73 and half C/73.

(Erase heading not required.)

Instructions regarding War Diaries and Intelligence Summaries are contained in F. S. Regs., Part II. and the Staff Manual respectively. Title pages will be prepared in manuscript.

Place	Date	Hour	Summary of Events and Information	Remarks and references to Appendices
NOYELLES	May 1st	—	Considerable shelling of our trenches to which we retaliated vigorously. Ammunition expended 149.	
—	2	—	Our batteries retaliated for enemy shelling. D/71 silenced an enemy battery. Various registrations carried out. Ammn expended 192.	
—	3	—	Retaliation again for enemy shelling our trenches. A working party dispersed. Ammn expended. 274	
—	4	—	B/70. C/70 + C/71 carried out a bombardment of the enemy's trenches, which did not draw much retaliation. D/71 again silenced enemy battery. Ammn expended 327	
—	5	—	Our trenches were heavily shelled which caused us to retaliate vigorously. Ammn expended. 427.	
—	6	—	Still heavy shelling of our trenches. C/70 dispersed a small working party. Our batteries carried out an organised bombardment between 5.5.40 p.m. which must have done much damage. Ammn expended. 1042.	
—	7	—	Large Minenwerfer very active on our trenches rest of day. C/71 shelled a working party with effect. Ammn expended 458.	

WAR DIARY or INTELLIGENCE SUMMARY

Left Group 15" Divl Artillery
HQ 71"B.A. A/71. B/71. C/71. D/71. Army Form C. 2118.
B + C /70 + C/73 + ½ D/73

Place	Date	Hour	Summary of Events and Information	Remarks and references to Appendices
FOTELLES	May 8	-	Battery positions at C & D/71 were shelled with 4.2's & 5.9's. D/71 dispersed a working party, and some obtained 4 direct hits on a machine gun emplacement. Amn expended – 294.	
-	9	-	Slight enemy shelling of our trenches to which we retaliated. A/71 blew in 3 loopholes in enemy front line. D/71 set a day-out on fire & dispersed a working party. B/71 damaged enemy parapet of front trench & wire. 6mm expended 6.20.	
-	10	-	Large minenwerfer discovered firing from behind DUMP. This was engaged by D/73. Amn expended. 369.	
-	11	-	Up to 3.45 pm every thing comparatively quiet. At 3.45 enemy started shelling our front trench which increased in violence. At 4.15 pm a mine was exploded and enemy bombardment became intense. Enemy attacked & took our front trenches on a front of about 300x. Our batteries were heavily shelled with 5.9's. We kept a barrage all through to guns. D/71 had direct hits in 2 pits, but no damage were done to guns, both of which were in action again with 2 or 3 hours.	

WAR DIARY
or
INTELLIGENCE SUMMARY.

(Erase heading not required.)

Army Form C. 2118.

LH Group. 15th Div: Artillery.

Place	Date	Hour	Summary of Events and Information	Remarks and references to Appendices
NOEULLES	11th	Continued	Gas shell was freely used by the enemy, and our layers & telephonists carried out their duties in smoke helmets for some 4 hours. Casualties. No 4100 Sargt Sampson C. A/71 wounded. No 81793 Gnr Suters J. C/71 wounded No 82750 Bmbr Flannagan B. C/71 wounded) No 94749 Corp Mitchell E. C/70. killed No 61387 Sargt Preece G.I.F. Ammn. expended 4182.	
"	12		We bombarded enemy trenches. Ammn expended 1660.	
"	13		A quiet day. Ammn expended 190.	
"	14		Our battery positions heavily shelled. Casualties M40984 Sgt Sellis BC. A/71 wounded. 9215 Dr Mee G. BAC/71. killed -78366 Gnr Williams G.H. B/71 died of wounds. -75403 Dr Lawrence W. BAC/71. 66294 Gnr Andrews BAC/71 and 59094 Gnr Sibley C B/71 all wounded. Ammn expended 2643. 61387 Sargt Preece G.I.F. 83367 Gnr Heal F. 10 3967 Gnr. Laws A. and 7941 Gnr Watts J.A all C/71 wounded. Ammn expended 2643.	

WAR DIARY
or
INTELLIGENCE SUMMARY

Army Form C. 2118.

Left Group 15th Divl. Artillery

Place	Date	Hour	Summary of Events and Information	Remarks and references to Appendices
NOVELLES	May 15	—	A quiet day. Ammn expended 118.	
"	16th	—	C/71 shelled in training - no damage done no casualties. Ammn expended 122.	
"	17th	—	Be carried out a bombardment of the enemies trenches South of Hohenzollern Redoubt. Enemies retaliation very heavy. Ammn expended 1263.	
"	18th	—	A quiet day. Ammn expended 86.	
"	19th	—	Our batteries retaliated to heavy trench mortar fire. Ammn expended 169.	
"	20th	—	A quiet day. Ammn expended 120.	
"	21st	—	A mine was blown up between Hohenzollern & the Quarries and our batteries opened barrage on the far lip. Ammn expended 405.	
"	22nd	—	A quiet day. Ammn expended 327.	
"	23rd	—	A mine was exploded near the Quarries otherwise a quiet day. 319. Ammn expended.	
"	24th	—	A quiet day. Ammn expended 365.	
"	25th	—	Hostile minenwerfer rather active. We threw ours at 9 P.m. and enemy retaliated rather heavily. Ammn expended. 155.	
"	26th	—	D/71 engaged a suspected OP. and registered 3 direct hits. A/rB/71 engaged loopholes with good results. Ammn expended. 327.	

WAR DIARY or INTELLIGENCE SUMMARY

Army Form C. 2118.

Left Group. 15th Divl. Artillery — Hqrs. 71, B/71, C/71, A/71, B/71, D/71, B/70 and C/70 and C/73

Place	Date	Hour	Summary of Events and Information	Remarks and references to Appendices
NOEULLES	27th	—	Hostile Artillery quite active all day. Our batteries kept them retaliating. Amm expended. 282.	
—	28th	—	Hostile trench mortars & field guns fairly active. Amm expended 8.69.	
—	29th	—	D/71 & B/70 reinforced by one section each from 64th B.S. 12" Siege. Amm expended 968	
—	30th	—	C/70 & C/71 reinforced by one section each from 64th B.S. A quiet day. Amm expended. 321.	
—	31st	—	A quiet day. Amm expended. 227	

J. W. Stirling Col. R.F.A.
Commdg. Left Group. 15th DA.
1.6.16

WAR DIARY or INTELLIGENCE SUMMARY

Army Form C. 2118.

June

71st Brigade R.F.A.

Vol 10

Place	Date	Hour	Summary of Events and Information	Remarks and references to Appendices
NOYELLES.	June 1st	—	Considerable hostile activity with hand & rifle grenades otherwise a quiet day. Amm. expended. 198.	
"	2nd	—	Enemy shelled our trenches with French mortars and light field guns. All heavy artillery seems to have disappeared. Amm. expended. 186.	
"	3rd	—	A quiet day. Amm. expended. 63.	
"	4th	—	Field guns again active on our trenches. Amm. expended. 136.	
"	5th	—	A quiet day. Amm. expended: 78.	
"	6th	—	A quiet day. Amm. expended: 36. D/71 became C/73, & C/73 became D/71 (now).	
"	7th	—	We engaged a trench from which rifles and machine guns were shooting at our aeroplanes. Hostile artillery much quieter. Amm. expend 109.	
"	8th	—	C/71 engaged more snipers loopholes, and two in 3. All batteries registers hostile wire. B/71 explodes a hostile bomb store. Amm. expended 167.	
"	9th	—	A quiet day except for slight hostile field gun activity. Amm. expended. 74.	
"	10th	—	We started building a dummy battery. Heavy shelling of Keep in part of A/71. Amm. expended. 46.	
"	11th	—	Put more full near battery. C/71 fired at working parties heard working in enemy front line. Amm exp. 74.	

Army Form C. 2118.

2.

71st Brigade R.F.A.

WAR DIARY
or
INTELLIGENCE SUMMARY.
(Erase heading not required.)

Place	Date	Hour	Summary of Events and Information	Remarks and references to Appendices
NOEULLES	June 12th	-	A quiet day. Amm. expended 43. Trench mortars and field guns fairly active.	
-	13th	-	Enemy shelled our communication trenches practically incessantly. Amm. expended 23.	
-	14th	-	Rifles and Machine guns were busy firing at our aeroplanes which were flying very low owing to clouds. Be engaged trenches concerned. Amm. expended 98.	
-	15th	-	Few amount of hostile shelling. Our batteries retaliated into selected points with good effect. Amm. expended 62.	
-	16th	-	Flashes were fired from our Cluny positions. Enemy immediately ranged on them by aeroplane with 4.2's. Amm. expended 50.	
-	17th	-	Hostile field guns very active. Our batteries retaliated onto selected points. Section at 1.85 & 8.5 : 40th Div: are thought together under their own battery Commanders. Various aeroplane registrations carried out. Amm. expended. 65.	
-	18th	-	H/r located a 4" gun in HAISNES. A quiet day. Amm: expended. 25.	
-	19th	-	Enemy shelled our communication trenches with field guns. C/71 disposed a large hostile working party. Amm. expended. 84.	
-	20th	-		
-	21st	-	Owing to an error it was reported that enemy were attacking. We opened heavy barrage. Amm. expd 200	

T2134. Wt. W708—776. 500000. 4/15. Sir J. C. & S.

WAR DIARY or INTELLIGENCE SUMMARY.

Army Form C. 2118.

71st Brigade R.F.A.

Place	Date	Hour	Summary of Events and Information	Remarks and references to Appendices
NOYELLES	June 22	-	Slight hostile shelling of our lines. Amm. expended. 58.	
"	23	-	A very quiet day. Amm. expended. 8.	
"	24	-	Our bombardment commences. B/71 cutting wire and the three batteries bombarding M.G. emplacements etc. Enemy retaliation very slight. Amm. expended. 430.	
-	25th	-	Wire cutting and bombardment continued. Various roads, communication trenches and trench tramways barrages all through the night. Amm. expd. 586.	
-	26	-	Wire cutting and bombardment continued. Amm. expended - 490.	
-	27th	-	Wire cutting and bombardment continued all during day. We fired in conjunction with raid at night with aid of gas, and barraged roads and communication trenches. Amm. expended 1910.	
-	28th	-	Wire cutting & bombardment continued. Amm. expended. 580.	
-	29th	-	Fired in support of trench raid by 48th Infantry Brigade. Wire found to be fairly well cut, but raiding party were held up by hostile bombs & trench mortar fire. Amm. expended 1869.	
-	30th	-	Wire cutting & bombardment continued. No infantry action taken. Amm. expended. 705.	

W. Hall, Lt. Colonel, R.F.A.
Commanding 71st Bde R.F.A.

CONFIDENTIAL.

War Diary

71st Bde RFA

From 1st to 31st July, 1916.

E Boyce
Major, R.A.
1st August, 1916.   Bde Major, 15th Divnl. Arty.

1st Army Form C2118
15 July
Vol II

T
71st Brigade, R.F.A.

WAR DIARY
or
INTELLIGENCE SUMMARY.
(Erase heading not required.)

July 1916.

Instructions regarding War Diaries and Intelligence Summaries are contained in F.S. Regs., Part II. and the Staff Manual respectively. Title pages will be prepared in manuscript.

Place	Date	Hour	Summary of Events and Information	Remarks and references to Appendices
NOYELLES	July 1st	—	33rd Division on our left carried out a raid of the enemy trenches. Our batteries cooperated with batteries of 33rd D.A. Ammunition expended 530 rounds.	
"	2nd	—	Our trenches shelled with 4.2's field guns and minenwerfers during the afternoon. Our batteries retaliated. Ammunition expended 94 rounds.	
"	3rd	—	During the afternoon and night, minenwerfers and 4.2 Howitzer shelled our Communication Trenches. Our batteries retaliated expending 86 rounds.	
"	4th	—	Field guns registered on trenches in the morning. A quiet afternoon. Ammunition expended 48 rounds.	
"	5th	—	4th Infantry Brigade carried out a successful raid on the enemy trenches. 3 prisoners brought back. Our batteries cooperated expending 400 rounds.	
"	6th	—	Hostile field guns and heavy howitzers bombarded our trenches west of the morning. Our batteries retaliated expending 100 rounds.	
"	7th	—	The usual field guns and trench mortars. Ammunition expended 38 rounds.	
"	8th	—	Heavy stuff on our trenches to the south of Brigade zone. Enemy has apparently made a raid. Our batteries co-operated expending 405 rounds.	
"	9th	—	Enemy blew a mine and was active with rifle grenades. Amm. expended 106 rounds.	

WAR DIARY or INTELLIGENCE SUMMARY

Army Form C. 2118.

71st Brigade R.F.A.

July 1916

Place	Date	Hour	Summary of Events and Information	Remarks and references to Appendices
NOEULLES	10th	—	A fairly quiet day. At 11.30 pm we blew a mine near the HOG'S BACK. Our infantry raided the enemy trenches taking dug outs and bringing back 2 prisoners. We barraged the enemy support trench & communication trenches expending 248 rounds.	
"	11th	—	Usual enemy trench mortar activity. C/71 knocked out a small pom-pom gun which was doing a great deal of damage to our snipers' plaks etc. This gun was located in or near the enemy support line. Ammunition expended 132 rounds.	
"	12th	—	Enemy field guns and trench mortars very active all day. Our batteries retaliated expending 156 rounds.	
"	13th	—	The enemy blew 2 mines, and fired the usual amount of trench mortars. We expended 138 rounds	
"	14th	—	Usual trench mortar activity. Otherwise a quiet day. Amm. expended 104 rounds	
"	15th	—	A few field gun shells fell on Quarry Bay & Reserve trench during morning. Afternoon quiet. Ammunition expended 138.	
"	16th	—	Started wire cutting and bombardment assisting 8th Div. on our left expending 5000 rounds	

Army Form C. 2118.

WAR DIARY
or
INTELLIGENCE SUMMARY.

(Erase heading not required.)

1/1st Brigade R.F.A.

July 1916.

3

Place	Date	Hour	Summary of Events and Information	Remarks and references to Appendices
Noyelles	July 17th	-	Enemy blew a mine near Quarries. We continued wire cutting and bombarding assisting 8th Div on our left expending later — at 8.45 enemy bombarded our trenches round the Border Redoubt with intense violence. We barraged round the redoubt. Enemy came across from Archer Sap and raided the Redoubt taking away 12 prisoners. Amm. expended 548 rounds.	
"	18th	-	Continued wire cutting and bombarding assisting 8th Div on our left expending 1972 rounds.	
"	19th	-	Programme continued expending 3000 rounds.	
"	20th	-	A quiet day. Ammunition expended 1014 rounds.	
"	21st	-	A quiet day. Relief orders arrive. Ammunition expended 76 rounds.	
"	22nd	-	First Sections pulled out of action at 4.30 pm relieved by 8th D.A. and march back to ANVIN. approx: 30 miles.	
ANVIN	23rd	-	Second Sections and Headquarters march back to ANVIN.	
"	24th	-	In billets at ANVIN.	
"	25th	-	In billets at ANVIN.	
MONCHEL	26th	-	Whole brigade march to MONCHEL — 17 miles.	
OUTREBOIS	27th	-	Whole brigade march to OUTREBOIS — 16 miles.	

WAR DIARY
or
INTELLIGENCE SUMMARY.

71st Brigade R.F.A.

July 1916.

Army Form C. 2118.

Place	Date	Hour	Summary of Events and Information	Remarks and references to Appendices
	July			
OUTRE BOIS	28	—	At Outrebois in billets.	
"	29"	—	At Outrebois in billets.	
"	30"	—	At Outrebois in billets.	
BETHEN- COURT.	31st	—	Marched to BETHENCOURT.	

J.W. Heath. Lt. R.F.A.
Commanding 71st Brigade R.F.A.

War Diary.
71st Brigade RFA.
1st — 31st July 1916.

15th Divisional Artillery.

71st BRIGADE

ROYAL FIELD ARTILLERY

AUGUST 1 9 1 6

CONFIDENTIAL.

WAR DIARY.

of

71st Brigade R.F.A.

From 1st August, 1916   to   31st August, 1916.

VOLUME Number 14

E Boyce
Major, R.A.
Brigade Major R.A., 15th Divisional Artillery.

Army Form C. 2118.

Vol 12

WAR DIARY 71st Brigade R.F.A.
or
INTELLIGENCE SUMMARY.
(Erase heading not required.)

August 1916

Place	Date	Hour	Summary of Events and Information	Remarks and references to Appendices
Bettencourt	1st	—	In billets at Bettencourt	
"	2nd	—	Marched to Beaucourt	
Beaucourt	3rd	—	First echelon of Batteries marched up to ALBERT and second East of ALBERT. Headquarters and second echelon in billets at BEAUCOURT.	
Albert	4th	—	Headquarters and second echelon march up to ALBERT. First echelon came into action East of MAMETZ WOOD relieving 19th D.A. W/31 Bdr. Read. A.8. B/71 wounded	
Caterpillar Valley	5th	—	Headquarters and second echelon came into action East of MAMETZ WOOD.	
"	6th	—	Headquarters heavily shelled with 8". B/71 have one gun knocked out. No 8002 Gnr. Stringwell G. B/71 and 9657 Sgt. Gooden 6.a B/71 wounded. Ammunition expended 604 rounds.	
"	7th	—	Headquarters heavily shelled with 8". B/71 have 5 men buried. No 9736 Gnr. Short W. B/71 killed. No 9159 Sgt. Sheppard E.A. B/71 accidentally killed. Ammunition expended 838 rounds. 9737 Gnr Dower E. B/71 and 64766 Dr. Bugler E. B/71 wounded.	
"	8th	—	Headquarters move back to North of MONTAUBAN. CATERPILLAR VALLEY shelled. Batteries harassed with 8" and 5.9" all night. Ammunition expended 1388	

Army Form C. 2118.

WAR DIARY **II**
or
INTELLIGENCE SUMMARY. 7th Brigade R.F.A.

August 1916

(Erase heading not required.)

Instructions regarding War Diaries and Intelligence Summaries are contained in F.S. Regs., Part II. and the Staff Manual respectively. Title pages will be prepared in manuscript.

Place	Date	Hour	Summary of Events and Information	Remarks and references to Appendices
Morlancourt	9th	—	Enemy barraged Ammunition Track with 5.9.0 at night intermittently. Our Batteries carried out bombardment of enemy trenches. No. 20 D.H. died. 769/71 and 8685 Gun Hooding. 6,769/71 wounded. Ammunition expended 1536 rounds	
"	10.		Our Batteries carried out continuous bombardment. Enemy Artillery rather quieter. Ammunition expended 2056 rounds	
"	11.		Enemy bombarded our trenches and BAZENTIN-LE-PETIT fairly heavily. Our Batteries continued, carrying out a part of the Intermediate Trench. At 10.30/pm Enemy Lancers captured part of Intermediate Trench. Ammunition expended 2800 rounds.	
"	12.		Batteries continued firing barrage. 8/71 flattened on a new work west of H164 Wood. Ammunition expended 3850 rounds	
"	13.		Barrage and other continued. A quiet day. Ammunition expended 2450 rounds	
"	14.		B/71 and Brigade Headquarters bombarded with shrapnel bursts of 4.2.0 from MARTINPUICH. No damage done. Ammunition expended 2450 rounds	

Army Form C. 2118.

August 1916.   71st Brigade, R.F.A.

WAR DIARY
or
INTELLIGENCE SUMMARY.
(Erase heading not required.)

Instructions regarding War Diaries and Intelligence Summaries are contained in F.S. Regs., Part II. and the Staff Manual respectively. Title pages will be prepared in manuscript.

Place	Date	Hour	Summary of Events and Information	Remarks and references to Appendices
Near Merlaton	15th	—	A fairly quiet day. 18/71 continued barraging enemy approaches to 57335 firing a close 8/71 wounded and the 78863 Gr H.R. Johnson 8/71 wounded. Ammunition expended 2865 rounds.	
	16th		92nd Division captured a portion of NEW TRENCH. Our guns covered the attack, expending 3650 rounds.	
	17th		A fairly quiet day. We continued usual barrages. Expended 2550 rounds.	
	18th		After a very heavy bombardment our troops captured HOLLAND HOUSE and 750 rounds HIGH WOOD and gained their objective. Lieut. R.M. Stockly and No 23541 Dr. D. Oxford 8/71 wounded. Ammunition expended 4550 rounds.	
	19th		Our barrage continued barraging. Otherwise a quiet day. Expended 1876 rounds. Sent out party to reconnoitre German wretch line which was found unoccupied as far as 500 yards behind Beving Cemetery attacked and occupied the Reserve Line at Coleng Line to himself. No 9174 Gr S. Clayton hurde killed. Ammunition	
	20th		149 Dewey 8/71 wounded. expended 3654 rounds.	

WAR DIARY or INTELLIGENCE SUMMARY.

Army Form C. 2118.

71st Brigade R.F.A.

August

Place	Date	Hour	Summary of Events and Information	Remarks and references to Appendices
near Montauban	21st		Enemy shelled CATERPILLAR VALLEY heavily expending on ammunition dump.	
	22nd		We continued our barrages expending 3658 rounds.	
	23rd		A heavy Artillery duel west of the day. Enemy shelled our trenches severely. Ammunition expended 3045 rounds.	
			16/71 very heavily shelled in morning over 100 5.9" falling within a radius of 100 yards. One direct hit on gun pit slightly damaging gun. 6.2513, Gnr. E. Hingley 8/71 & 96586 Bdr. Englefield 8/71 wounded. Ammunition expended 3465 rounds.	
	24th		Brigade Headquarters heavily shelled with 8" A.P. No damage done. Batteries continue barrages and were on night attack by 3rd Brigade which failed expending 3684 rounds.	
	25th		Enemy shelled neighbourhood of Batteries with 5.9" and gas shell. Ammunition expended 3586 rounds.	
	26th		Very heavy shelling of CATERPILLAR VALLEY and MAMETZ WOOD with 5.9", 4.2, and gas shell. No damage to Brigade whatever. Batteries continued barrage and assisted in attack on	

WAR DIARY or INTELLIGENCE SUMMARY

Army Form C. 2118.

I 7th Brigade R.F.A. August

Place	Date	Hour	Summary of Events and Information	Remarks and references to Appendices
Near Abeele	26 (cont)		Splendid line by 1st Brigade which was successful. Ammunition expended 4005 rounds.	
"	27th		Hants wood and valley heavily shelled with H/Vs & 5.9's during morning. Otherwise a fairly quiet day. We carried out usual bombardments expending 2450 rounds	
"	28th		A quiet day. Ammunition expended 2165 rounds	
"	29th		Our batteries fired barrage in conjunction with during attack which was cancelled at last moment owing to unfavourable weather. Expending 2850 rounds.	
"	30th		Very wet & windy day. Consequently very little shooting. Enemy made a small counter attack on Puritch line with bombs which broke down. Ammunition expended 2465 rounds	
"	31st		A fairly quiet day. Enemy shelled ammunition track with 5.9's. Observing balloons caused no damage. We engaged large parties of the enemy shewing himself into front result. Ammunition expended 2468 rounds.	

W.H. Heath Lt.Col.
Comdg 7th Bde R.F.A.

CONFIDENTIAL.

War Diary

of

71st Brigade, Royal Field Arty.

From 1st September, 1916 to 30th September, 1916.

Volume Number 15

Major, R.A.
Bde Major 15th Divisional Arty.

Army Form C. 2118.

Vol 13

1st to 30th September 1916. WAR DIARY or INTELLIGENCE SUMMARY. 71st Brigade R.F.A.

Place	Date	Hour	Summary of Events and Information	Remarks and references to Appendices
	Sept.			
Mt Hatauba	1st	—	A quiet day. Ammunition expended 3640 rounds	
"	2nd	—	One section of B/71 & D/71 move back to FRECHENCOURT. Usual barrages continued. Ammunition expended 3250 rounds.	
	3rd	—	Headquarters and second sections of B/71 and D/71 move back to FRECHENCOURT. Usual barrage continued. Amm. expended 2465	
	4th to 10th	—	Headquarters, B/71 & D/71 in billets at FRECHENCOURT. Usual day and night barrages continued by A/71 & C/71. Average ammunition expenditure 2500 rounds per day.	
	11th	—	First section B/71 and D/71 recalled to action, and come into action East of CONTALMAISON. B/n Hippisson A/71 slightly wounded.	
	12th	—	Second sections B/71 and D/71 come up to East of CONTALMAISON. Nothing to report. Gnr Jay A/71 slightly wounded.	
	13th	—	All four batteries bombarding enemy's positions day and night, expending 4860 rounds.	
	14th	—	Bombardment continued. Very little hostile retaliation. Ammunition expended 4924 rounds.	

Army Form C. 2118.

WAR DIARY
or
INTELLIGENCE SUMMARY.

1st September to 30th September 1916

71st Brigade R.F.A.

(Erase heading not required.)

Place	Date	Hour	Summary of Events and Information	Remarks and references to Appendices
	Sept 15th	—	Division attacked at 6.20 A.M. and took objectives ie outskirts of MARTINPUICH by 6.A.M.: F.O.O.'s were pushed up close with the assaulting waves, and did good work in answering the enemy SOS out of the villages. At 3 p.m. the whole will age with 400 prisoners was in our hands. Hostile artillery fire quite slight. Amn. expended 4865.	
	16th	—	All batteries busy reconnoitring forward positions & returning to report.	
	17th	—	Batteries moved forward — D/71 to North of MAMETZ WOOD A/71 + C/71 to North of BAZENTIN LE PETIT B/71 to East of CONTALMAISON. New registrations etc carried out.	
	18th	—	A/71 & D/71 heavily shelled but no forward over had been dug by 500m new [?] was done. All batteries engaged enemy guns (spotted by seen [?] [?] from newly found guns). A/71. dislodges a German observer in the Church tower of LIGNY TILLOY	
	19th	—	German Counter attacks on TRUE TRENCH replies Barraged to line of communications day + night. Ammunitie expended 4865 rounds.	

Army Form C. 2118.

WAR DIARY
1st September to 30 September 1916

INTELLIGENCE SUMMARY
71st Brigade R.F.A. III

(Erase heading not required.)

Place	Date	Hour	Summary of Events and Information	Remarks and references to Appendices
	Sept.			
	20th	—	Headquarters relieve 13th Headquarters A/71 & C/71 go back to Saint GRATIEN to billets. Nothing to report. Ammunition expended 20 6.5 rounds.	
	21st & 22nd		Various registration carried out. Infantry skirmishes pour MARTINPUICH in which some ground was gained and a few prisoners taken.	
	23rd		B/71 advances his battery position by 1000 yards to North of HAMEL WOOD. D/71 flattens out a portion of trench occupied by the enemy. Ammunition expended 28 6.5 rounds.	
	24th	—	Usual harrasing barrages. Nothing to report.	
	25th	—	2nd Lieut R.S. PEARSE killed (D/71) shot by a sniper [illeg] MARTINPUICH 20 4.8 rounds Both batteries in Counter Battery Duty during small local attack	
	26th-28th		Nothing to report. Usual barrages continued.	
	29th		Lieut J.K. DACRE & Serjeant H/O 71st Brigade wounded in Right Eye when visiting O.P.'s just East of MARTINPUICH. DESTREMONT FARM captured. D/71 fired 30 rounds H.E. into this farm & both of this Farm 30 Hum Just before we took it. Gnr MASTERS B/71 killed while working on telephone lines	

151638E September 1916 WAR DIARY 71st Brigade RHQ Army Form C. 2118.

Place	Date	Hour	Summary of Events and Information	Remarks and references to Appendices
CONTALMAISON	Sept 30th		No. 19107 L SHEPHERD Agus 7th Bedfs Liniman wounded. Lieut J.K DACRE died at No 2 Field Ambulance MERICOURT, from wounds received in action on 29/9/16.	

EWHeath Lt Col RFA
Comdg 71st Brigade RHA

30/9/16

CONFIDENTIAL.

War Diary

of

71 Bde RFA

1st October, 1916. to 31st October, 1916.

VOLUME. 16

E Boyce

Major R.A.

Brigade Major 15th Divisional Arty.

Army Form C. 2118.

4th Brigade RFA

Vol 14

WAR DIARY
or
INTELLIGENCE SUMMARY
(Erase heading not required.)

Instructions regarding War Diaries and Intelligence Summaries are contained in F. S. Regs., Part II. and the Staff Manual respectively. Title Pages will be prepared in manuscript.

Place	Date	Hour	Summary of Events and Information	Remarks and references to Appendices
CONTALMAISON	1-10-16		During the night the attack was active but not very heavy. The enemys artillery was active this morning especially on PRUE & STARFISH trenches. Prior to the attack on the FLERS-LESARS front and support line by the 23rd Division Infantry whom we were supporting, we carried out the bombardment ordered. The attack was successful. Our FOOs reported parties of the enemy in M11C. who were fired on and dispersed. During the day we fired 373 A9, 520 A.X, 139 7.8.x and 37 incendiary shells. 2 Hostile (Wombs) fired at Brigade Hd qrs near 12 S.K. Baere (exact ?grounds)	
	2-10-16		The enemy were very quiet along our front during the day. We also did very little firing as the light was very bad. There are no items of interest to report. We fired 168 4.A, 365 A.X, 203 B.x mostly on organised barrages.	
	3-10-16		The enemy were again very quiet. We continued firing our night barrage until about 11 a.m. as light was again too bad for observation. We fired 641 A, 403 A.X, 81 13.x & 100 PF	
	4-10-16		With the exception of a few 77"s + 4.2s in X6C + S1d the enemys artillery was again quiet. We carried out the ordered bombardment and when 523 A, 899 A.x, 203 13.x. The Brigade began here moved to X17B near Shamrock trench, not a very nice place and seriously shelled.	
	5-10-16		Except for intermittant shelling of MARTINPUICH the enemy artillery were very quiet. all 3 howitzer was seen firing from M11c78 this was engaged by 60 pdr battery We fired 558 A, 240 A.x + 65x. Gns Meadows 4 APL 9oo was reported missing.	
	6-10-16		The enemy artillery today again were very active today they shelled our front and support line heavily with 4.2 farts. The enemy were reported in the slow work of LESARS, these were engaged. D/71 in dipping him new Position. the MARTINPUICH-BAZENTIN road had a shell one of them fell being McMan Wounding ?.	The ??

WAR DIARY / INTELLIGENCE SUMMARY

71st Brigade R.F.A. — Army Form C. 2118.

Place	Date	Hour	Summary of Events and Information	Remarks and references to Appendices
	6-10-16 (cont)		The names are as follows No 4178 Gr Passmore T. Killed. – 14896 Bdr Galvin A.H. wounded – 103415 Bdr Thomas T. " – 141491 Bdr Eagle H. " – 39519 Gr Hague G. " – 7822 Lyr Gilmour T. " – 57732 Gr Shaw F. " 2/Lt W. Goodman joined brigade and attached to C/71 2/Lt C.A. Pike & Williams " " B/71	
	7-10-16		We fired during the day 6349, 532 AX. Wa Go Wagon Lines moved to X16a At 1.45 p.m. the 23rd Div attacked LE SARS. We supported their attack & carried out the bombardment ordered. Both ground and air observers reported that our barrage was excellent and very effective. The 23rd Div gained their objective but the 47th Div did not. During the night the enemy shew considerable activity. We expended 2824A 920 AX & 1037 BX.	
	8-10-16		There was heavy hostile artillery activity during the morning. His developed into an attack on the Canadians who were driven back of the DESTREMONT Line. We fired 4819, 299 AX & 80 BX. C/71 with one section of A/71 relieved A/103. They took over their line in situ. D/71 relieved D/104 " " " " " " "	[9-10-16]

WAR DIARY or INTELLIGENCE SUMMARY

Army Form C. 2118.

1/1st Yorkshire RHA

Date	Hour	Summary of Events and Information	Remarks and references to Appendices
9-10-16		MARTINPUICH was shelled intermittently during the day. We have Hinman Bombardment Keany out and expended 473A & 227AX. 2/Lt. C.O.C. Marshall joined the brigade and was attached to B/71.	
10-10-16		During our daily bombardment we expended 360A, 336AX, 032 Bx. 2/Lt W Sm See A/71 was killed by shell fire at A/71 Battery position, buried at X12a.central. A/71 moved its section back from C/71 amn. train one section after him. Is this section transferred to M32 c.65.2. Drivers Griffiths and Welsh A/71 awarded military pts. B/71 moved 1 section during the night to S2a 43.9	
11-10-16		The enemy artillery was very active around MARTINPUICH. We carried out the usual bombardment and expended	
12-10-16		The 9th Division attacked the WARLENCOURT LINE and failed. We bombarded as usual firing	
13-10-16		There was exceptional activity on the part of the enemy artillery today. We fired. Capt. Fitzwilliam A/71 awarded military Cross.	
14-10-16		Enemy parties around LE PART WOOD were shelled with very good results. He fired 224A, 668AX, 643 Bx & 21 PF Shells. Her artillery was very heavy Tr. he fired	
15-10-16		Capt. Patten from Alley A/71 took over military duties. Very severe shelling by enemy during the day and very little seen movement today. Pacaman Harding wire was knocked out. He bombarded and fired 517A, 536AX, 349 Bx during the day.	
16-10-16		One section of each Battery was relieved by 70 Bde today. Enemy artillery again active especially in COURCELETTE and Gilbert trench. We fired all hours etc 40A, 444AX, 92 Bx	

WAR DIARY
or
INTELLIGENCE SUMMARY

Army Form C. 2118.

71st Bde R.F.A.

Place	Date	Hour	Summary of Events and Information	Remarks and references to Appendices
ST GRATIEN	17.10.16		The relief by 70th Bde was completed about noon. The billets handed to ST GRATIEN.	
	18.10.16 to 26.10.16		We were in rest billets at ST GRATIEN. Colonel Heath A.M.S. & Capt Fitzwilliams Mr proceeded on leave to England. Capt Russell Lts Ratcliffe Beacon & Perrin return went to Paris!!! We were called up hurriedly to relieve 73rd Bde which to be complete by noon 28th inst	
BAZENTIN le PETIT	27.10.16		moved to 73rd AA Gp at BAZENTIN Zero's section went into action today	
	28.10.16		Our relief complete at noon with the exception of Col. Heath C.M.G. who had not come back from leave. We took over guns "in situ". We fired 20A 102Bx during the day. The enemy were fairly quiet. We took over the 118 Siege Battery 6"hows.	
	29.10.16		The enemy were active today especially around MARTINPUICH. Two enemy aeroplane were flying very low over LECARS & WARLENCOURT. To 8pm we fired 259A, 449Ax 402Bx. Chi had one man killed & one wounded with their lone gun.	
	30.10.16		The harassing-carrying off the enemy was continued as usual. We bombarded as usual we fired 374A, 170Ax, 146Bx, 31Bsk, 75F.	
	31.10.16		An exceptionally busy day on the front of the enemy. They were enemying with 77s with some success our parties working in the open. We carried out bombardments about firing 508A, 81Ax, 333Bx, 168F.	

MCHeath Lt-Col R.F.A.
Comdg 71st Brigade R.F.A.

CONFIDENTIAL.

War Diary.

of

71st Bde R.F.A.

From 1st November, 1916 - 30th November, 1916.
VOLUME 17

1.11.16.

Gallagher Captain,
for Bd Major 15th Divisional Arty.

Army Form C. 2118.

Vol 15

WAR DIARY
INTELLIGENCE SUMMARY
(Erase heading not required.)

Place	Date 1916	Hour	Summary of Events and Information	Remarks and references to Appendices
BAZENTIN-le-PETIT	1/11/16		Hostile Artillery was exceptionally active today about 3.30 p.m. they bombarded our trenches in front of LESARS with 4.2's and 5.9's. One enemy aeroplane was brought down. The relief of 15th Division Infantry by the 48th Div (South Midland) commenced today. We carried out the usual bombardments and expended 315A, 206Ax, 204Bx, 39BSk, 307F. Four officers were attached to the brigade Lt NE Haig to A/71, 2nd Lts Parker & Davies to C/71 + 2nd Lt Kavanagh to D/71	
	2-11-16		The enemy gunners were again active today and paid special attention to the neighbourhood of EAUCOURT L'ABBAYE. We fired 36 1A, 319 Ax, 224 Bx, 39 BSk, 32 F.	
	3-11-16		LE SARS and PRUE trenches were heavily shelled during the day also the Tidby line from HIGHWOOD. Enemy aircraft were exceptionally active one of our planes was brought down at the back of Bois Loupard A/253 who attended to him for ¾ hr (slow Sundays). He bombarded and used 258 A, 26 2Ax, 183 Bx + 77 F.	
	4-11-16		Enemy still acting as feelers up an ammunition dump at M12C at F3omm. a bad day the Shrewsbury. More bombarded GALLWITZ TRENCH with satisfactory results during the day we fired 369 A, 355 Ax, 247 Bx 68 BPF + 95 F.	
	5-11-16		Had carried out the relief bombardments toward the attack on BUTTE de WARLENCOURT and GIRDLINES. Zero hour was at 9.10 am and 50th Div attacked but were driven out by enemy counter attack, attention was not at all clear all day. Enemy put up a strong barrage on SNAG TREANCH for 10 minutes. We shot at and dispersed several enemy parties in M.4, 5.46. During the day we fired 1150 A, 504 Ax, 613 Bx + 337 F.	
	6-11-16		Foot inspection air shooting very good. LE SARS, MARTIN PUICH + EAUCOURT L'ABBAYE were intermittently shelled throughout the day with 4.2's + 5.9's he shot 382 A, 243 Ax, 256 Bx + 154 F during H day. Capt Fitzallevens MC returned from leave. 2nd Lt HT Vizard O/71 Awarded Bar to Military Cross.	

WAR DIARY / INTELLIGENCE SUMMARY

Army Form C. 2118.

Place	Date	Hour	Summary of Events and Information	Remarks and references to Appendices
	7-11-16		Enemy fairly quiet throughout the day. We dispersed an enemy working party at G.36.a.3.5. We fired K54 A, 103 Ax, 85 Bx + 30 F shrapnel shells. Cpl Bailey H.Q. wounded (shell) (right hand?)	
	8-11-16		Bombardment and harassing carried out as ordered. Enemy carried out a real bombardment and shelled heavily behind the line. Enemy batteries were annoying. We shot 647 A, 196 Ax, 918 Bx + 53 F during the day.	
	9-11-16		Enemy retaliated on BAUCOURT & MARTINPUICH from bombardment. We dispersed several enemy parties during the day. We fired 306 A, 182 Ax, 101 Bx, 104 F. D/71 went on outer out of action today and proceeded to PIERREGOT.	
	10-11-16		Our 18 pdr batteries to take over position of 330 Bde tonight. B/71 are going into the position they had already dug in M.17 central. D/71 relief complete. Canadians attacked at midnight, we fired 290.9, 178 Ax 50 Bx + 20 F during day.	
	11-11-16		The night was very had all day pairing, we carried out the ordinary bombardments and fired 30 A, 30 Ax + 51 F during the day.	
	12-11-16		Night again bad. Enemy artillery very active all day between LE SARS & EAUCOURT L'ABBAYE from the direction of LOUPARD & BAPAUME. We shot 341A, 124 AB, 113 Bx Siege Battery. Easy the nights we carried our command.	
	13-11-16		We had a bombardment at 5.45 am arranged during the night. 5th Army attacked Nº 1 Area and took 60 officers & 3000 o.r. prisoners. Lt Atkin re turned from leave. We shot 553.5 A + 177 Ax during the day. B+C batteries registered on new	
	14-11-16		Lt Nicholson went on leave 2/Lt G. McKillum came as O.O. 23rd DA took over from 4th DA. Shelled (?) had numerous calls for Trenfchate (Others Crpts). We fired 354 A + 270 Ax.	

2449 Wt. W14957/M90 750,000 1/16 J.B.C. & A. Forms/C.2118/12.

Army Form C. 2118.

WAR DIARY
or
INTELLIGENCE SUMMARY

(Erase heading not required.)

Place	Date	Hour	Summary of Events and Information	Remarks and references to Appendices
In the field	15-11-16		A very quiet day 678A and 262Ax expended	
	16-11-16		The Highwood Tramway was intermittently shelled. We carried out a usual barrage firing 986A and 210 AX. M5-a.2.2. naval barrage A 361, Ax 233 fired A/71 started an enemy op on M5-d.2.2. naval barrage	
	17-11-16		6 Saps and Transept intermittently shelled. B/71 had their horses blown up. Capt C.E.P Henderson being killed. Lt A/W Deacon and 2nd Lt R.G Farrington were wounded but remained at duty. B/71 are going to move back to our posn M2.6.F2	
	18-11-16		Very quiet day. Tramway shelled as usual. Canadians on our left took five (5) prisoners. Ban Sapera B/71 killed in Martinpuich Rd to fire usual barrage expending 776A and 635 AX.	
	19-11-16		Martin Percy was shelled with S.O.S and S.I. Capt K. Willett was posted to the Brigade Command B/71 the area usual firing and expended 457A - 347Ax firing barrage out a usual. We shot 457Ax 450A.	
	20-11-16			
	21-11-16		655A 493 Ax	
	22-		623 " 391 "	
	23-		245 " 471 "	Naval barrage carried out
	24-		160 " 207 "	nothing of interest to report
	25		186 " 284 "	
	26		136 " 167 "	
	27		136 " 273 "	
	28		168 " 233 "	
	29		168 " 469 "	
	30		168 " 1650 "	

CONFIDENTIAL

WAR DIARY

of

71st Brigade R.F.A.

From 1st December, 1916 to 31st December, 1916.

VOLUME 18

Major, R.A.
Brigade Major 15th Divisional Artillery.

Confidential
15. D.A.

Herewith War Diary for
71st Bde R.F.A. for month
of Decr 1916.

31-12-16.   Styhom.
           Cmdg 71st Bde R.F.A
                    Lt Col R.F.A

WAR DIARY or INTELLIGENCE SUMMARY

Army Form C. 2118.

Vol/16

71st Bn R.F.A.

Oct 1916.

Place	Date	Hour	Summary of Events and Information	Remarks and references to Appendices
BAZENTIN LE PETIT	1st		Very quiet day – 7 o.g.g.f. Chereneton Imprecable.	Oct.
	2nd		The MARTIN PUICH & LE SARS very heavily shelled all day & at intervals during the night. We strafed all approaches at intervals both night & day	A/17
	3rd		Lt Col H Heath C.M.G. ceased to Command 71st Bn. Lt Col C.S.T.M. INGHAM assumed Command. Enemy active. MARTIN PUICH heavily shelled. B/73 Bty R.F.A. Posted to Y1 2nd Bn R.F.A. under the command of MAJOR R. F. G. READAM. D.S.O., M.C.	A/17
	4th		We strafed enemy strong points, roads & tracks etc. Enemy rather less active than usual.	A/17
	5th		We strafed wire which had been repaired by the enemy on our front. Numerous small working parties were successfully strafed. Enemy artillery very quiet	
	6th		Enemy artillery very active firing at all of our trenches in turn. MARTIN PUICH and LE SARS being heavily strafed. Very quiet night.	A/17
	7th		We shelled LOUPART Wood & found a M.2 Bty which was firing	

WAR DIARY
or
INTELLIGENCE SUMMARY

Army Form C. 2118.

Place	Date	Hour	Summary of Events and Information	Remarks and references to Appendices
BAZENTIN LE PETIT	7th		along the MARTIN PUICH – EAUCOURT Rd. we also relieved Roads which to as usual.	App 1
	8th		Relieved in the Line and marched to Rest Billets at PIERREGOT	
	9th			
	10th			
	11th			
PIERREGOT	12th			
	13th			
	14th		In Rest Billets	
	15th			
	16th			
	17th			
	18th			
	19th			
	20th			
	21st			
	22nd			App 1
	23rd		Took over the line from 10th Bn R Fus – Zone QUARRY E. M.4 b 33. Hostile artillery active all day. A weeks during the night. We fired on Certain of his trenches in our zone, & watered some working Parties.	App 1
	24th			

Army Form C. 2118.

WAR DIARY
or
INTELLIGENCE SUMMARY

(Erase heading not required.)

71st Bde R.F.A.

Instructions regarding War Diaries and Intelligence Summaries are contained in F. S. Regs., Part II. and the Staff Manual respectively. Title Pages will be prepared in manuscript.

Place	Date	Hour	Summary of Events and Information	Remarks and references to Appendices
[Lower Billing?] HOOD	25th	12.10 am	We strafed the enemy for 10 minutes with Gas & H.E. Shell, and repeated this several times during the day. Enemy quiet.	M14
	26th		We strafed several strong points and trenches. Roads etc in our zone. 9 caught a working party on which we inflicted casualties. Enemy artillery quiet.	M14
	27th		We bombarded trenches in our zone. Enemy very busy with 77° & 4.120 on our support line. One Round of our Battery [illegible] successfully drove off an Enemy Plane.	
	28th		We kept enemy trenches and Strong Points under intermittent firing all day. Enemy very active with 5.9 & 9.8 inch on our and support line all day. MARTINPUICH being shelled with Gas Shell during the evening	

2449 Wt. W14957/M90 750,000 1/16 J.B.C,& A. Forms/C.2118/12.

WAR DIARY or INTELLIGENCE SUMMARY

71st Bde RFA Dec 1916

Place	Date	Hour	Summary of Events and Information	Remarks and references to Appendices
LOWER Wood	29th		We fired on enemy trenches intermittently throughout the day and caused casualties to several working parties seen during the day. Enemy artillery active.	
	30th		Fired as on 29th. C/70 (attached to 71st FBde) successfully drove off 8 hostile planes flying over La Barque.	
	31st		Very quiet night. Enemy very active with guns of all calibres on our front. Considerable movement seen on the BAPAUME Rd, and several men were killed there by our batteries. A 77 mm gun at M6c32 was seen and knocked out by C/71, several direct hits being obtained an ammunition dump near this gun was blown up with the first round.	

31-12-16.

W Ryan.
Lt Col RFA
Cmdg 71st Bde RFA

Confidential.

War Diary

of

71st Brigade R. F. A.

1st January 1917 - 31st January 1917.

VOLUME 19

E. Boyce

Major, R.A.

Brigade Major 15th Divisional Artillery.

Army Form C. 2118.

WAR DIARY
or
INTELLIGENCE SUMMARY
(Erase heading not required.)

Y/2/BdeR.F.A.

January 1916   Vol 17

Place	Date	Hour	Summary of Events and Information	Remarks and references to Appendices
Lower Wood	1st		Enemy shelled Seven Elms, Northupost with 4.2's & 5.9's. We shelled enemy front line trenches & approaches during the day. ~~Enemy trench mortars & artillery fairly active during the day.~~ ~~Trench Mortars silenced on several occasions~~. Enemy working party v. M.G. emplacement effectively shelled. Enemy batteries in Brigdem active during the night.	A.C.
	2nd		Two enemy 77mm. Batteries engaged & silenced during day. D/71 obtained direct hit on enemy O.P. Enemy Artillery active from direction of trenches during day. Heavy enemy shelling during night silenced by B/71 & C/71.	A.C.
	3rd		Hostile Artillery very quiet. Bad visibility. We shelled enemy's front line trenches & supports.	A.C.

Army Form C. 2118.

WAR DIARY
or
INTELLIGENCE SUMMARY

(Erase heading not required.)

71st Bde. R.F.A.

January, 1917

Place	Date	Hour	Summary of Events and Information	Remarks and references to Appendices
Lower Wood	4th		We bombarded Enemy front line & approaches during the day. Bad visibility.	LC.
	5th		Slight hostile shelling from Gueudecourt during the day. We shelled hostile working parties causing casualties & bombarded enemy front line trenches. Enemy shelled Le Sars & Martinpuich intermittently with 5.9's from direction of Loupart Wood & Grevillers.	LC.
	6th		We shelled enemy working parties & trench approaches. Direct hits were obtained on gun position by our batteries causing casualties. Enemy active during the day.	LC.
	7th		We shelled enemy's front line trenches & communications. Martinpuich & Flers line slightly shelled with 4.2's during the day.	LC.

Army Form C. 2118.

WAR DIARY
or
INTELLIGENCE SUMMARY

71st Bde. R.F.A.

January 1917

Place	Date	Hour	Summary of Events and Information	Remarks and references to Appendices
Louis Wood.	8th		Our Artillery shelled Enemy's front line Trenches & working parties, causing some casualties.	IC
			Two enemy 77 m.m. batteries engaged, & silenced for the remainder of the day.	
			Hostile Artillery very active all day. Martinpuich heavily shelled with 5.9's from direction of Bazentin. 7th & 8th Battalion H.Q.rs also receiving some attention.	
	9th		We bombarded enemy's Trenches intermittently during the day & shelled working parties; causing casualties.	IC
			Hostile Artillery fairly active during the day. mainly 4.2's.	
			Our Artillery searched the ground behind the enemy's front lines during the night.	
	10th		We shelled enemy's front lines & approaches & inflicted casualties on working parties.	IC
			Hostile Artillery shelled L.E.S.a.Rs & Flers Line intermittently during the day with 4.2's.	

Army Form C. 2118.

WAR DIARY
or
INTELLIGENCE SUMMARY
(Erase heading not required.)

January 1917 71st Bde R F A

Place	Date	Hour	Summary of Events and Information	Remarks and references to Appendices
Lower Wood.	11th		We bombarded enemy's front lines & approaches. Bad visibility. Hostile artillery fairly quiet.	XC
	12th		We shelled the enemy's front trenches & dispersed some working parties. Hostile artillery fairly quiet.	XC
	13th		Our Artillery bombarded the enemy's front line Trenches & approaches in conjunction with the Heavies. Enemy shelled LE SARS & EAUCOURT L'ABBAYE with 5.9's intermittently during the day. Bad visibility & 4.2.5	XC
	14th		We shelled the enemy's front line & supports during the day. Hewitson reported enemy to have to have [been] Enemy shelled howitzers in counter in counterbattery shooting my LC	XC

Army Form C. 2118.

WAR DIARY
or
INTELLIGENCE SUMMARY

January 1917   21ˢᵗ Bde. R.F.A.

Place	Date	Hour	Summary of Events and Information	Remarks and references to Appendices
Lesars Wood	15ᵗʰ		Our Artillery were active all day. Two hostile batteries were silenced during the afternoon & working parties dispersed with casualties. Enemy shelled Le Sars & Crescent alley with 5.9's & 4.2's. Burst of rifle shells falling in Le Sars were duds.	I.C
	16ᵗʰ		We bombarded enemy's front line Trenches & approaches. Hostile Artillery very quiet all day. Visibility bad.	I.C.
	17ᵗʰ		Our Artillery shelled the enemy's front lines - tracks behind. Hostile artillery quiet.	I.C
	18ᵗʰ		We bombarded enemy's front trenches & approaches. Hostile Artillery shelled Martinpuich, Le Sars & Bancourt Z' Abbaye with 5-9's intermittently during the day.	I.C
	19ᵗʰ		Our Artillery shelled enemy's front line & tracks behind, & dispersed working parties with casualties at M.12.a. Usual hostile shelling of Martinpuich & Le Sars with 5.9's.	I.C

2449 Wt. W14957/Mgo 750,000 1/16 J.B.C. & A. Forms/C.2118/12.

Army Form C. 2118.

WAR DIARY
or
INTELLIGENCE SUMMARY.

January 1917.   71st Bde.   RFA

Place	Date	Hour	Summary of Events and Information	Remarks and references to Appendices
Little Wood	20th		We shelled enemy's front line trenches & dispersed some working parties. At M.11.c.8.6 we set fire to a very light group which burnt for 15 minutes. Hostile artillery shelled Martinpuich – Bazentin L'Abbaye intermittently with 4.2's from direction Zenone Wood & Gueudecourt. At 1 p.m. Le Sars was heavily shelled with shrapnel for 10 minutes.	L.C.
	21st		Our artillery bombarded enemy's trenches & approaches according to programme. Hostile artillery fairly active all day. Le Sars & Destremont Farm were shelled intermittently with 4.2's & Shrapnel. The R.H. Avenue N.1 & 26th Avenue – Butterfret alley with 5.9's & 4.2's. 77mm – Butterfret alley with 5.9's & 4.2's.	L.C.
	22nd		We bombarded enemy's front lines & supports. B/71 & C/71 silenced a 77mm Battery in M.6.c. Hostile artillery shelled Le Sars Martinpuich – Warlencourt with 5.9's – 4.2's. The Hun hit & 26th Avenue were shelled from direction of Gueudecourt. Shelling ceased upon retaliation. Bad visibility all day.	L.C.

WAR DIARY or INTELLIGENCE SUMMARY

Army Form C. 2118.

January 1917. 71st Bde. 12 F.A.

Place	Date	Hour	Summary of Events and Information	Remarks and references to Appendices
Leuze Wood	23rd		Our Artillery shelled the enemy's front line & approaches, executing some good wire cutting. Visibility very bad. 6/71. at 6.30 p.m. the Right Battn Hdqrs. was heavily shelled by the enemy with 5.9's & 4.2's. for 3 minutes from the direction of Bouleaux, otherwise hostile Artillery very quiet.	LC
	24th		We bombarded the enemy's front trenches & supports. Some working parties were dispersed. Hostile artillery fairly active. Sailisel & Hautrypuich being heavily shelled with 5.9's & 4.2's from direction of Lesars & Bouleaux. Our batteries had some effective wire-cutting.	LC
	25th		Our artillery shelled the enemy's front line & support trenches & continued some effective wire cutting. Visibility bad. Martinpuich & Sailisel farm were intermittently shelled by 5.9's during the day, from the direction of Bouleaux & Le Sars & two line were shelled with 4.2's, direction uncertain.	LC

Army Form C. 2118.

WAR DIARY
or
INTELLIGENCE SUMMARY

(Erase heading not required.)

January 1917.   71st Bde. R.F.A.

Place	Date	Hour	Summary of Events and Information	Remarks and references to Appendices
Lower Wood.	26th		Our Artillery shelled enemy's front lines & carried out an area search. Wire cutting being continued & gaps kept open. We silenced a battery in M.G.C. at 3.30/—. Hostile artillery fairly active. Martinpuich being shelled by 77m. battery from the direction of Bys. & Bapaume 102— with shrapnel.	L.C.
	27th		Our Artillery bombarded enemy's front lines & caused casualties amongst enemy troops M.17.a.0.8. to M.17.a.4.7. at 10.30/— Lewis guns also caused casualties in same area at 9.30 — any probable relief. Hostile artillery normal. Visibility good.	L.C.
	28th		We shelled the enemy's front trenches & supports during the day. Hostile artillery active. Martinpuich, Gun line & Rutherford Alley being heavily shelled with 5.9's from the direction of Lonfaut Wood & P9s.	L.C.
	29th		Our artillery shelled the enemy's front lines & approaches. Hostile artillery fairly quiet. The Bapaume Rd. was searched with 77m. & 4.2.5 from the direction of Lonfaut Wood at 5.pm. Visibility bad.	L.C.

Army Form C. 2118.

WAR DIARY
or
INTELLIGENCE SUMMARY

(Erase heading not required.)

January 1917   71st Bde. R.F.A.

Place	Date	Hour	Summary of Events and Information	Remarks and references to Appendices
Loren Wood.	30th		At 1.45. am. we carried out a successful raid on the Butte de Warency. Three machine guns & teams was disposed of, two being trench mortar was destroyed or team captured or killed. Two dugouts smashed up & set on fire, one was large & contained a Company of seventeen Prisoners were captured. A large number of Germans were killed. Our own casualties were slight, not exceeding seventeen in all. At 3:30 am. a loud explosion was heard in the Butte, – at 1 pm. dense smoke was still coming out of Butte. Throughout, the hostile artillery was very J. At 2.16 am. a 77. m. Battery was silenced in M.G.C.3.30. by B/71 & C/71. At 1.15 pm. 26 Avenue & Spencer Trenches were heavily shelled by 77 m. & 4.2's from Loupart Wood. During the afternoon Wilhelm Alley & O.G.1. was heavily shelled with 5.9's & 4.2's from Luigny Trolley – Bresielles.	L.C.

Army Form C. 2118.

WAR DIARY
or
INTELLIGENCE SUMMARY

71st Bde. R.F.A.

January 1917 *(Erase heading not required.)*

Instructions regarding War Diaries and Intelligence summaries are contained in F. S. Regs., Part II. and the Staff Manual respectively. Title Pages will be prepared in manuscript.

Place	Date	Hour	Summary of Events and Information	Remarks and references to Appendices
Leuze Wood	31st		Our Artillery bombarded enemy's front line & approaches at 10 a.m. O/71 blew up a large bond store at M12.a.o.6. Hostile Artillery fairly quiet. Intermittent shelling of Le Sars, Destrement farm, & Martinpuich during the day with 4.2" & 77 mm from the direction of Loupart Wood. Visibility good.	Ze

31/1/17

M.Berry? Major
Commdg.

2449 Wt W14957/M90 750,000 1/16 J.B.C. & A. Forms/C.2118/12

CONFIDENTIAL

WAR DIARY

OF

71st. BRIGADE R.F.A.   15th. DIVISIONAL ARTILLERY

FOR MONTH OF FEBRUARY 1917.

VOLUME XX

E.Bogee Maj. R.A.
for Brig:General.
Commanding 15th. Divisional Artillery.

Army Form C. 2118.

Vol 18
71st Bde. R.F.A.

WAR DIARY
or
INTELLIGENCE SUMMARY

(Erase heading not required.)

February 1917

Place	Date	Hour	Summary of Events and Information	Remarks and references to Appendices
Loupart Wood	1st		We bombarded the enemy's front line trenches & approaches and dispersed working parties in M.5.d.6.0. & M.5.d.5.2. Hostile artillery active during the day & night. Le Sars, Ybus Lane & William Alley being heavily shelled with 5.9's & 4.2's from direction of Loupart & Grévillers. Martinpuich & area south of Martinpuich intermittently shelled with 5.9's & 77m.m. from direction of Loupart Wood.	LC
	2nd		Our Artillery shelled the hostile front line & supports. Several enemy aeroplanes over our lines, one of which was bad, hostile artillery quiet during morning, but unusually active later. Martinpuich, O.5.1. William Alley, LE SARS, 26 Avenue, DESTREMONT FARM, & RUTHERFORD ALLEY shelled with 5.9's & 4.2's from direction of Loupart Wood & GRÉVILLERS. Bursts of fire on BAPAUME ROAD & FAUCOURT from 77 m.m. battery.	LC

2449 Wt. W14957/M90 759,000 1/16 J.B.C. & A. Forms/C.2118/12.

Army Form C. 2118.

WAR DIARY
or
INTELLIGENCE SUMMARY

(Erase heading not required.)

HQrs. 71st Bde RFA   February 1917.

Place	Date	Hour	Summary of Events and Information	Remarks and references to Appendices
LOWER WOOD	3/2/17		Our artillery carried out their programme and fired on the enemy front line as well as our smoky Avg. outs and OPs. During the morning 26 Avenue & William alley were shelled by 5.9.1 from Grenilles. Later in the day Martinpuich was heavily shelled for a short time with 77mm from Eaucourt L'Abbaye & Kenora Road, also receiving our attention with 4.5s. Observation impossible in the afternoon.	WD
	4/2/17		Our artillery again fired on the enemy front line and searched back. Hostile artillery normal. M27a 70.90 to M26 & 70.30 was shelled at intervals with 77mms from M6c 1.2. Visibility bad. No movement observed.	WD
MIRVAUX	5/2/17		HQrs moved out to MIRVAUX and BARRACKS, to PIERREGOT. Considerable delay occurred owing to the late arrival of the 2 Aust BA'S who relieved us.	WD
"	6/2/17		At MIRVAUX — nothing to report.	WD
	7/2/17		" nothing to report.	WD

Army Form C. 2118.

WAR DIARY
or
INTELLIGENCE SUMMARY

(Erase heading not required.)

HQ 11 R'BDE FA February 1917

Place	Date	Hour	Summary of Events and Information	Remarks and references to Appendices
MIRVAUX	5/2/17		Nothing to report	SR?
	6/2/17		Nothing to report	SR?
	10/2/17		Nothing to report	SR?
	11/2/17		Nothing to report	SR?
	12/2/17		Nothing to report	SR?
	13/2/17		Nothing to report	SR?
	14/2/17		Nothing to report	SR?
	15/2/17		Nothing to report.	SR?
OUTREBOIS	16/2/17		HQrs and Batteries moved to Outrebois via Talmas & Fieux court	SR?
BEAUVOIR-SUR-CANCHE	17/2/17		HQrs and Batteries moved to Ligny-sur-Canche via St Ouen & Grand Vicoin L'Hôpital & Vacquerie & Rouy	SR?
S'MICHEL	18/2/17		HQ & and Batteries moved to S' Michel via PPL	SR?
	19/2/17		BGC reporting to VI Corps III Army. Nothing to report	SR?
	20/2/17		Advanced party of Officers and signallers under Major Graham C/41 - went to Arras	SR?

WAR DIARY
or
INTELLIGENCE SUMMARY

Army Form C. 2118.

HQr 71st Bde RFA   February 1917

Place	Date	Hour	Summary of Events and Information	Remarks and references to Appendices
St MICHEL	21/2/17		Nothing to report	NTR
"	22/2/17		Working party came & were to prepare positions for Batteries	NTR
ARRAS	23/2/17		HQrs moved to ARRAS. 2 sections of each C and D Batteries came up into action in defensive positions in ARRAS	NTR
"	24/2/17		Nothing to report.	NTR
"	25/2/17		C & D Batteries registered. Observation difficult.	NTR
"	26/2/17		C & D Batteries continued registration. One section of B Battery came up into action at ARRAS. C & D Batteries assisted in a successful raid upon the enemy trenches made by the 12th Divn. 28 prisoners taken.	NTR
"	27/2/17		The two remaining sections of B Battery came up into action. Our artillery fired a few rounds on various points in the enemy lines. Hostile artillery normal.	NTR
"	28/2/17		B Battery registered, and the other Batteries fired bursts of hostile artillery not very active.	NTR

28/2/17   (signed) Arthy Mackinnon Lt. Col.
Commd'g 71st Bde RFA

CONFIDENTIAL

War Diary

of

91 Bde R.F.A.

From 1st March 1917   -   To 31st March 1917

Volume 21

WAR DIARY
or
INTELLIGENCE SUMMARY

Army Form C. 2118.

HQrs 11th Bde R.F.A.   March 1917   Vol 19

Place	Date	Hour	Summary of Events and Information	Remarks and references to Appendices
ARRAS	1/3/17		Hostile Artillery quiet except for occasional shelling of trenches in B9a with 4.2" from direction of FEUCHY. S.O.S. lines and dispersal of our Artillery barrage registration. H.19.C.3.1 Large working parties seen. Hostile working party of H.19.C.3.1 Large working parties seen. N.U.C. Poor visibility most of the day. Our Artillery carried on intermittent bombardment.	
"	2/3/17		Hostile Artillery very quiet. Visibility again bad owing to mist, and the at 2.0 p.m. afternoon.	
"	3/3/17		Hostile Artillery – French historians decreased rounds from the Cambrai Orb's Roads. Our own Artillery registered a hostile party in the Railway Triangle. Visibility poor.	
"	4/3/17		Hostile Artillery fired a number of 77mm & 5.21 into the Cemetery in the morning, apparently at enfilading enemy working parties. Our artillery dispersed a few working parties. Visibility good.	
"	5/3/17		Hostile Artillery placed a heavy barrage in the morning along the line B.29.d.4.4. to C.29.b.6.2. from the direction of ATHIES. All batteries were used up to 5.9's. Our artillery fired last at observation gain.	

Army Form C. 2118.

WAR DIARY
or
INTELLIGENCE SUMMARY

(Erase heading not required.)

HQ 4th BARFA   March 1917.

Place	Date	Hour	Summary of Events and Information	Remarks and references to Appendices
ARRAS	6/3/17		Hostile artillery retaliated for our bombardment mainly with T/M's at 11.10 am. Our bombardment was apparently quite effective. Many enemy aeroplanes & T.A. guns active but not effective. Visibility good. Concentrate bombs shelling J sub support line in the afternoon.	
"	7/3/17		Hostile Artillery very quiet. A few shells fell in the country between 8.0 and 9.0 am. Our artillery active and some wire cutting and also dispersed a party in the Railway Triangle. Visibility poor.	
"	8/3/17		Hostile Artillery opened a heavy barrage on our front & support lines at 8.40 am, and at 8.45 am. a small raid was attempted by the enemy & enemy gun the section J.W.16. The raid was completely repulsed. Our Artillery dispersed a large working party in Hindenburg trench during the morning. But this had some T.M. & M.G. party, and at cease work until about 11.10 am. Hor Artillery in reply. Visibility good except during flypasts at 7.30 am.	
"	9/3/17		Hostile Artillery quiet. A T.M. at 6.10 AM was active during the day. Artillery active own gun Artillery wire cutting continues. Visibility good — no movement seen on Brigade Front.	

WAR DIARY or INTELLIGENCE SUMMARY

Army Form C. 2118.

HQ Arm 41 B'de R.F.A.   March 1917

Place	Date	Hour	Summary of Events and Information	Remarks and references to Appendices
ARRAS	10/3/17		Hostile Artillery quiet. Our Artillery continued wire cutting, but visibility was not overly bright.	OP
"	11/3/17		Hostile Artillery very much more active, ARRAS being shelled at various times throughout the day with shells of varying calibre - up to 8". B Battery was very heavily shelled with 4.2's, 5.9's & 8" from the direction of FEUCHY during the afternoon. This continued until 6.0 pm. Our artillery continued wire cutting & fire at the TRIANGLE. Counter-battery registration carried out by D Battery. Visibility good. Bn. Brown of W/41 Staff killed at 2/41.	OP
"	12/3/17		Hostile Artillery activity again above normal. From 1.15pm to 3.45pm E28a shelled with 8" from direction of FEUCHY. At 11.0 am E29b was shelled with 8". Harrassing fire until ? Our artillery continued wire cutting and engaged accurate amount of enemy movement, notably from STATION to 6.65am in HERMIES TRENCH & S. side of RAILWAY TRIANGLE. At 8.0 an ? FEUCHY remaining up for about 10 minutes.	OP

WAR DIARY or INTELLIGENCE SUMMARY

Army Form C. 2118.

HQ "Y" Bty RFA March 1917.

Place	Date	Hour	Summary of Events and Information	Remarks and references to Appendices
ARRAS	13/3/17		Hostile Artillery quiet in the morning. At 12.5 pm Right Battalion Front heavily shelled with shell of all calibres until 5.50 pm. Our artillery continued wire cutting and covered the T.M's in their wire cutting. Enemy party of 15 or 16 fired at and dispersed at 5.22 pm. S.O.S signal was sent up in front of Cemetery upon which our artillery opened fire on their D.O.S lines, ceasing at 5.52 pm. Observation difficult on account of mist.	SD7
	14/3/17		Hostile Artillery shelled the Cemetery between 11.0 am & 11.40 am with 4.2 & 5.9 mm. About 3.0 pm our trenches 2 of the Cemetery heavily shelled with 4.2, 5.9 & 5.9 T.M's active later. Our artillery active, various during day on hostile trenches, & covering our T.M's. B/140 carried out action with our tactical visibility post.	SD7
	15/3/17		Hostile artillery shelled F.26 617 with 4.2 from 8.10 am to 9.0 am. Trenches on our right shelled during the morning with 77mm. Early in the morning (5.10 am) a bombardment began on our

WAR DIARY or INTELLIGENCE SUMMARY

Army Form C. 2118.

HQ Hev. H. Bde RFA   March, 1917.

Place	Date	Hour	Summary of Events and Information	Remarks and references to Appendices
ARRAS.	15/3/17 (continued)		right and our Artillery opened fire promptly in reply to SOS. Some movement was fired at late + wire cutting continued. Night good. One action of each C/41 + D/41 relieved by A/40 + B/40 respectively.	SOS
	16/3/17		Hostile artillery quiet on our front. We carried out wire cutting as usual. Visibility poor. Relief of C/41 + D/41 completed. All parties from all batteries returned to ARRAS to continue work on new Positions. OC Br Chishe of 40 Bde RFA took over tactical command of the Group at 10.0 a.m.	SOS
	17/3/17		Work continued on new Battery Positions	SOS
	18/3/17		Work continued on new Battery Positions	SOS
	19/3/17		Work continued on new Battery Positions.	SOS
	20/3/17		2/Lt McGuire, Capt Holloway of 24 killed by a 4.2. 2/Lt McGuire of the same Battery also killed + 2 wounded. A/41 C/41 + D/41 all came up into action in their forward positions	SOS

Army Form C. 2118.

WAR DIARY
or
INTELLIGENCE SUMMARY.
(Erase heading not required.)

Instructions regarding War Diaries and Intelligence Summaries are contained in F. S. Regs., Part II. and the Staff Manual respectively. Title pages will be prepared in manuscript.

HQ 41" B" R.F.A.   March 1917.

Place	Date	Hour	Summary of Events and Information	Remarks and references to Appendices
ARRAS.	21/3/17		Hostile artillery heavily shelled the Division on our right at 5.0 a.m. Much movement seen in the early morning, especially abt Hermes Trench. B/71 & D/71 registered. Visibility good.	
	22/3/17		Carried out Wire Cutting with B/71. Watch attention chiefly directed on CEMETRY.	A/OFisher
	23/3/17		Continued Wire Cutting. Enemy artillery in our front line very active.	1117
	24/3/17		Engaged several Enemy Batteries on "Wireless" calls. Continued wire cutting. Hostile T.Ms active on our front line again.	1117
	25/3/17		B/71 heavy shells with 8". 2 guns knocked out and ammunition set on fire. Eye't for 8" enemy artillery gun.	1117
	26/3/17		B/71 did not fire. Vacinity P.O.R. Cemetery intermittently shelled all day with 77o and 4.20	1117
	27/3/17		B/71 did not fire. Enemy artillery active all day. Whole of 15th Div front shelled intermittently. T.Ms also very active	1117

Army Form C. 2118.

WAR DIARY
or
INTELLIGENCE SUMMARY.
(Erase heading not required.)

HQ 71st Bde R.F.A.   March 1917.

Place	Date	Hour	Summary of Events and Information	Remarks and references to Appendices
ARRAS	28/3/17		Observation good. Enemy Artillery fairly quiet during the morning, a few shell being fired at G.24.c.5.9 and in the vicinity of the cemetery. In the afternoon - hostile artillery was very active against ARRAS causing many casualties.	94.
	29/3/17	At 4:10 am an SOS signal went up on our front. Our batteries opened fire, but checked off considerably on the request of the infantry in order to make fire of a retaliatory nature & not barrage. ARRAS was shelled intermittently with 4.2" & 5.9" throughout the day. Hostile artillery and trench mortars were very active. ARRAS Station was shelled most of the day. B Battery observed were cutting and was shelled during the morning by balloon observation. At 4.0 pm, the enemy put over gas shell.				M.
	30/3/17			M.
	31/3/17		Wire cutting continued. Enemy infantry retaliated actively. HARAS received a good deal of trench mortar & hostile artillery. Movement in hostile lines engaged. Observation good. Agt was heavily shelled in the evening with 5.9". No casualties but many rounds of ammunition destroyed.	94.

Lieut. Col. R.F.A.
Commdg. 71st Brigade R.F.A.

C O N F I D E N T I A L.

War Diary

of

Y/1 Bde R.F.A.

VOLUME 72

From 1st April 1917 , 30th April, 1917.

Army Form C. 2118.

WAR DIARY
or
INTELLIGENCE SUMMARY.

(Erase heading not required.)

15 Div

No 7/St Bn RSR   April 1917.   JR 20

Place	Date	Hour	Summary of Events and Information	Remarks and references to Appendices
ARRAS	1-4-17		A hostile Aeroplane was shot down in ARRAS during the morning. B/71 wire cutting gun was heavily shelled all day with 59's. It is thought a hostile balloon was observing. Enemy artillery and trench mortars active. The station Cemetery, railway + rue St SAUVEUR received most attention. Our Artillery continued wire cutting.	W
	2-4-17		Enemy artillery fairly quiet, with the exception of about 350 59's B/71 wire cutting gun - which was damaged. Our artillery continued wire cutting + registration with good results.	W
	3-4-17		A quiet day - probably owing to bad light. Considerable movement was seen in enemy's lines at 7.0 a.m. Our artillery fired only 27 in registration ps	W
	4-4-17		First day of Bombardment (V day) Our Trench Mortars appeared to do excellent work. Batteries were cutting wire + the day - with the exception of two pauses ordered by DA in order that aeroplane photos might be taken. The enemy took advantage of these pauses to retaliate on ARRAS, but seemed when the Bombardment commenced. The enemy occasionally puts over a few gas or incendiary shell.	W

WAR DIARY or INTELLIGENCE SUMMARY

Army Form C. 2118.

71st Brigade R.F.A. n.l

April 1917

Place	Date	Hour	Summary of Events and Information	Remarks and references to Appendices
ARRAS	5/4/17		Second day of bombardment (w. day) A practice creeping barrage took place at 7.0 a.m this morning, but detailed corrections could not be made owing to fog. Enemy aircraft inactive. Retaliation poor. Two raids on hostile trenches by this division took place, which 71st Bde R.F.A. helped to support. Results not yet known.	
	6/4/17		Third day of bombardment (x day) 44 & 46 Infy Brigades carried out a raid in the morning. Our artillery went on with their programme as ordered. Hostile artillery active along the whole front from 6.0 a.m - 11.0 a.m. and generally increased activity was shown throughout the day. Several horses being set on fire. Enemy seemingly nervous sending up many "golden rain" rockets.	op
	7/4/17		Fourth day of bombardment (y day) - 1 day being postponed. The same programme was carried out by our artillery as on x day except that we had no practice barrage. The "12" Divn raided in the beginning again by our artillery. Hostile artillery now active again taken up at Ray.	op

WAR DIARY
or INTELLIGENCE SUMMARY

Army Form C. 2118.

April 1917.

H.Q. "Y" "72" Bde R.F.A.

Place	Date	Hour	Summary of Events and Information	Remarks and references to Appendices
ARRAS	8/4/17	Y Day	Our Artillery continued the bombardment according to programme, hostile Artillery not very active.	S.P.
	9/4/17	Z Day	The attack commenced at 5.30 a.m. Our artillery supplying by a creeping barrage after an intense bombardment. The enemy front support lines were quickly captured - our 3 ne being from C.24.d. to the Railway. A short halt was made on a line running E. of FREDS WOOD and then our Infantry advanced further to a line running roughly N + S through I.26. Central. The final point reached during the afternoon was the Himalaya Trench in H.28. Our own Infantry being ahead of that on either flank. Shortly after midday our Artillery commenced to move forward from ARRAS - C/71 - sustaining very severe losses from shell fire, both in men + horses, just before commencing the march. A halt was made for the night in H.19. Ad. Qrs being at H.26.f. Whilst carrying out a reconnaissance in the afternoon - Major Evans C/71, Major Begg D/71 + 2nd Lt. Whitehead D/71 refilled a 77 m.m. gun from various parts obtained promoters guns in the captured battery area, fired about 50 rounds at the enemy at a range of 700 yds.	S.P.

WAR DIARY or INTELLIGENCE SUMMARY

(Erase heading not required.)

Army Form C. 2118.

HQ. Y. "Z" 2d RFA.

April 1917

Place	Date	Hour	Summary of Events and Information	Remarks and references to Appendices
H.26.d.	10/4/17		A further infantry attack was made in the early morning by the 37th Div – our our infantry having been withdrawn. This was partly successful, the line was advanced to within a short distance of MONCHY LE PREUX. Our batteries moved up viz: H.28.a.; B/71 being the first Bty to arrive and this Bty and C/71 opened fire at 6 p.m. The weather conditions were very bad and we all the ground rendered movement the guns almost impossible.	NP
	11/4/17		Our Infantry advance little further and captured MONCHY LE PREUX, supported by our Artillery & our own Infantry. supp.d. also by Cavalry. in the attack.- supp.d. also by Cavalry.	NP
FEUCHY.	12/4/17		Very little advance was made during the day. Artillery fired at movement and also supported an attack N.E. of MONCHY which was not lasting successful. Our own infantry went out in the morning and were relieved by the 17th Div. Hd. Qrs. moved to H.27.d near FEUCHY.	NP
	13/4/17		Our Artillery fired at movement. A/71 destroying a considerable amount of transport. We commenced to consolidate the line. Our front line now runs Bty from H.30.d.8.8. to H.36.a.8.0. then along the road to MONCHY. The German front line from I.25.c.6.8. to I.31.a.11.	NP
	14/4/17		Our artillery fired at movement in various places. Hosti artillery active shelling our forward with 4.2" & 5.9" and gap shell danger. Enemy air reported to our from I.25.c. central to I.31.a. central Our artillery and aircraft shooting on account bad visibility. MONCHY & FEUCHY shelled & intermittently Enemy	NP
	15/4/17			NP

WAR DIARY or INTELLIGENCE SUMMARY

Army Form C. 2118.

HQ 4 72nd R.F.A.

April 1917

Place	Date	Hour	Summary of Events and Information	Remarks and references to Appendices
FEUCHY	16/4/17		Our artillery continued quiet at moment. Weather improving very cold. Hostile artillery normal - Hostile aircraft intervals by 4.21 + T.9.5. Our waggon lines moved back to OG. Battery positions in BRAY. Heavy gun limbers & teams in BATTERY VALLEY. Major J.R. Fitzwilliam AVM to take 2 Batty. RMA Collection RC normal. Hostile artillery quiet in the day very poor. MONCHY & FEUCHY shelled Even the day.	np
"	17/4/17		Our artillery again did not do much shooting. Visibility again poor. Hostile artillery very active. Total number of prisoners taken by Third Army since April 9th 195. Officers 5061 OR. 139 guns. 168 machine guns. 51 TM's.	np
"	19/4/17		Hostile artillery fairly active MONCHY shelled till 4 in the forenoon, FEUCHY CHAPELLE & CAMBRAI ROAD shelled with 4.2's & 5.9's. At irregular intervals.	np
"	20/4/17		Hostile artillery again active shelling the battery positions & FEUCHY. Several further casualties occurred to our men.	np

Army Form C. 2118.

WAR DIARY
or
INTELLIGENCE SUMMARY.
(Erase heading not required.)

HQrs 172nd R.F.A.

April 1917.

Instructions regarding War Diaries and Intelligence Summaries are contained in F.S. Regs. Part II. and the Staff Manual respectively. Title pages will be prepared in manuscript.

Place	Date	Hour	Summary of Events and Information	Remarks and references to Appendices
FEUCHY.	1/4/17		1st day. Our artillery carried on the bombardment on the whole front. The 45" I.B. Front preparatory barrage intended attack by the 15th Divn. Hostile artillery very active - scattered gas shelled all night.	OP
"	2/4/17		2nd day. Our artillery continued their programme. Hostile artillery again very active chiefly with heavies, causing a considerable number of casualties amongst our batteries.	OP
"	3/4/17		3rd day. The attack commenced at 5.30 am and our infantry attacked their 1st objective which was a line running roughly from Observed Enemy O.14 central to O.14.d.20. Owing to lack of support on the flanks they had later on to fall back to some extent, and occupied the recent German front line.	OP
Near MONCHY a/NILLE &c	4/4/17 →		Brigade moved up at 12.20 am to positions near LE FOSSES FARM. B/H sustaining severe casualties during the operation at 5.0 pm an attack was made on the line abandoned on the previous day and this was carried out with almost complete success except that CAVALRY FARM - on the CAM BRAI ROAD was not taken. Very heavy hostile barrage throughout the whole attack. Again very	OP

A 5834. Wt. W.4973. M.687. 755,000. 8/16. D. D. & L. Ltd. Forms/C.2118.

Army Form C. 2118.

WAR DIARY
or
INTELLIGENCE SUMMARY.   HQ ~ 11 "BDE. RFA
(Erase heading not required.)   April 1917

Place	Date	Hour	Summary of Events and Information	Remarks and references to Appendices
Near MONCHY at N.11.a.5.2	25/4/17.		Our new tent was erected under a patch of herbage put up by us. Hostile artillery active. B/71 & D/71 moved to other positions - being under observation in the res Hey held.	SVP
"	26/4/17		Batteries spent much of their time in improving their positions. An attack was made on CAVALRY FARM at 10.30 pm supported by us, but was only partially successful. Hostile artillery subsequent to active but A/71 heavily shelled at intervals.	SVP
"	27/4/17.		Hostile artillery normal. Our own artillery carried out a bombardment according to programs. 15th Divl Infantry again relieved - this time by 56th Divl Infantry.	SVP
"	28/4/17.		Hostile artillery active. A/71 & D/71 shelled at intervals throughout the day with 4.2"s & 5.9"s. Our artillery assisted in a bombardment covering an attack by the army on our Left.	SVP
"	29/4/17.		A/71 & D/71 again shelled at intervals - especially the former. Our own artillery fire was mainly directed at movement. Several enemy batteries DS 1/4.	SVP

Army Form C. 2118.

WAR DIARY
or
INTELLIGENCE SUMMARY.

(Erase heading not required.)

HQ 41st Bde RFA

April 1917

Place	Date	Hour	Summary of Events and Information	Remarks and references to Appendices
Near MONCHY le PREUX at N11 a 5.2.	30/4/17		A/41 again shelled heavily - chiefly with 5.9's at intervals throughout the day. Our own artillery only fired at moments in the daytime and carried out their programme at night. Total Brigade casualties during the month of April Killed 2 Officers 4 OR Wounded 3 Officers 118 OR Total Killed 57 Wounded 121.	

A Myhanworth
30/4/17 Comdg 41st Bde RFA

CONFIDENTIAL.

WAR DIARY

of

71ST BRIGADE R.F.A.

from 1st May, 1917.   to 31st May, 1917.

(Volume 23).

WAR DIARY or INTELLIGENCE SUMMARY

Army Form C. 2118.

Vol 21
HQ 41st Bde RFA

May 1917

Place	Date	Hour	Summary of Events and Information	Remarks and references to Appendices
Near MONCHY LE PREUX at N.11.a.5.2.	1/5/17		Hostile artillery normal. Our artillery confined to fire mainly on hostile movement. Lt Col Singham took over command of the Left Sub-Group - from Lt Col Christie 240 Bde. 58th Bde Infantry Left Sub-Group, from Lt Col Christie 240 Bde. 58th Bde Infantry came up on our front.	AP
"	2/5/17		Hostile artillery again active - especially against 241st Brigade & gas shelling stronger in N.11.a.	AP
"	3/5/17		The 56th Divn commenced an attack at 3.45 am. supported by us. The objective was the "Red Line" which ran roughly from the Bois au Vert to St Rohart Factory. This was part of an attack on a large scale by the 1st 3rd & 5th Armies. As far as our front was concerned, the attack was unsuccessful. Some portions of the objective was gained, but abandoned later in the day. Our batteries fired on their SOS lines at 8.10 pm in response to signals.	AP
"	4/5/17		On the whole a quiet day. Hostile artillery not very active in the morning but more so later in the day, shelling the neighbourhood of L'Fosse. Just now with SOS. In the evening 9/41 threw up gas shells. At 1.30 p.m. the VILLAGE DUMP in ARRAS was blown up - also 2 HQrs waggon lines. The equipment & material.	AP

WAR DIARY or INTELLIGENCE SUMMARY

Army Form C. 2118.

Month and Year: May 1917

HQ 4 1700 RFA

Place	Date	Hour	Summary of Events and Information	Remarks and references to Appendices
Near MUNCHY & PREUX at N.11.a.5.2	5/5/17		Hostile artillery fairly quiet during the day, but more active in the evening. Our artillery fired at movement with some success on the enemy. At 10.45 pm an SOS signal was sent up on the right of our front, and we opened fire - shortly dying down. Fire ceased about 11.0 pm when the signal of enemy moving about. Visibility moderate throughout the day.	
"	6/5/17		Hostile artillery somewhat more active than usual. Our own artillery fired at movement & caused several D/41 destroyed an MG emplacement in the evening & caused casualties to the enemy. It opened the same battery carried out a bombardment of LEONARD TRENCH. Visibility fair. 5/4 withdrawn to Y and relieved by the infantry.	
"	7/5/17		Hostile artillery again normal. In the early morning our How. carried out a bombardment of TOC TRENCH as required by the infantry. The day they bombarded FACTORY & LEONARD TRENCHES. At 5.0 am our row was extended further northwards to the new firing line roughly through the Nr R R of N VERT. 7L 153 Bde RFA also came under control of the Defoliated Group of this Town. Firing was carried on at night as usual on tracks & roads in enemy country.	

WAR DIARY
or
INTELLIGENCE SUMMARY.

Army Form C. 2118.

HQ 4 Bde FA

May 1917

Place	Date	Hour	Summary of Events and Information	Remarks and references to Appendices
Near MONCHY LE PREUX at N11a.5.2.	7/5/17		Hostile Artillery very quiet - a few 77mm on CAVALRY TRENCH at 12.30 p.m. Our artillery only fired at enemy. Visibility very poor.	App
"	8/5/17		Hostile Artillery quiet. FEUCHY CHAPELLE shelled with 5.9's from 7.9 from 12 noon until 2.30 pm. GEMAPPE shelled intermittently at 4.22 & 5.9's. Our artillery only fired at movement. Visibility poor up to 11.30 am. improving later.	App
"	9/5/17		Hostile Artillery active on N11+12, chiefly 5.9's. Gas shell in DIII in the early morning. In the evening aeroplanes shelling from on 5.9's. Our Arty carried out a successful shoot on TOOL TRENCH at midday. The Bosche fired on the movement caused by the shoot. Our artillery fired in response & an SOS call about 11.15 pm. Visibility fair.	App
"	10/5/17		Hostile Artillery rather more active. Our Artillery maintained harassing fire on the enemys back areas and restricted fire with the 4.5 How on TOOL TRENCH. At 6.30 pm the 168" Inf Bde carried out an attack on TOOL TRENCH which was reported. The attack was successful and the objectives were obtained with 16 casualties. N of Northern end of TOOL TRENCH & H11 came up into action in the evening, ^ going out. Hostile Artillery normal. Our Artillery carried out a programme of harassing fire on tracks in the enemys lines.	App
"	11/5/17		TOOL TRENCH At 3 pm went out for a few days rest and 412 NJ came up into action. HM moved to C.41 south with early morning.	App

CONNOLLY Lt. Col og Command,

Army Form C. 2118.

WAR DIARY
or
INTELLIGENCE SUMMARY.

(Erase heading not required.)

May 1917   HQ 173ᵈ R.F.A.

Place	Date	Hour	Summary of Events and Information	Remarks and references to Appendices
Near MONCHY PREUX & NINE A.2	13/5/17		Hostile artillery quiet. GORDON ALLEY & CAMBRAI ROAD receiving the most attention. MONCHY, GUEMAPPE & WANCOURT also receiving a few 5.9's. Our artillery again carried out harassing fire on hostile approaches in the enemys lines. DTM opn fired on the Northern part of TOOL TRENCH.	S/7
"	14/5/17		Hostile Artillery below normal. At 3.15pm MONCHY & TOOL TRENCH received some shelling. We fired on the hollow and J TOOL TRENCH now known as HOOK TRENCH- throughout the day. RFC engaged enemy aeroplanes & hostile battery at 9.10 pm with success. Visibility good.	S/7
"	15/5/17		Hostile Artillery shelled CHERISY Farm MONCHY GUEMAPPE & WANCOURT sharply with 5.9's. Shrapnels throughout the day. Our artillery carried out their high firing on roads tracks & bivouac fires at WI Sec ARTOIS. Visibility poor.	S/7
"	16/5/17		Hostile Artillery much more active. 6 POSTS from RIFLE TRENCH SAP were shelled with all calibres at intervals throughout the day, area shelled with all calibres at intervals throughout the day. DTM. fire on Ken Sapout causing several casualties. Visibility good.	S/7
"	17/5/17		Hostile Artillery below normal. GUEMAPPE & WANCOURT shelled during the morning. No movement seen. Our Artillery continued harassing enemy roads & tracks. Lt Gt INGRAM returned to command HQ 3ᵈ & also took over Left Sub Group.	S/7

Army Form C. 2118.

WAR DIARY
or
INTELLIGENCE SUMMARY.
(Erase heading not required.)

HQ 4th BARPA

May 1917.

Place	Date	Hour	Summary of Events and Information	Remarks and references to Appendices
HQ MERCATEL & PREUX au NILASZ	18/5/17		Hostile artillery normal. GUEMAPPÉ & WANCOURT - also the valley in N14 shelled at intervals. Our artillery fired at movement B/141 N14 occurred again in the open at Orgn and also caused new casualties. Patches of the enemy in the open. At 9.20 pm the enemy in the new trench (T67.3a) carried out a bombing attack on the northern part of T00l trench, supported by our artillery. This was not successful. New disposition being encountered than was expected.	SR
	19/5/17		Hostile artillery quiet. Occasional rounds on O7cxd O14d & O15cxd in the valley heavily shelled in the afternoon. Our artillery fired at movement & caused a number of hits on personnel moving in the open near U.3 en Arbor. Several of the Fallows at. and began their approach. On artillery supported an unsuccessful attack on Stirling Visibility good at 9.0 pm.	SR
	20/5/17		Hook & LOW & TRENCHES Hun shelled between Y14 & an by 9/2 & 4 gun. Hostile artillery normal. Hun patrol racey the Y14 - T00 m on night out. Our artillery supported an attack made to find & exploit. The heavy claim plan at 5.15 am. This attack gained 50 the nearest form report 19/5/17. trough down of Fallows. Visibility poor.	SR
	21/5/17		Hostile artillery rather more active. Our artillery fired at movement. Visibility fair 56th Div Infantry relieved by 31st Div.	SR
HQ RKS	22/5/17		15th DIV Artillery came out to rest at 6.0 pm. 2nd Div are being taken over by the 12.8A. H.Qrs moved to waggon Lines also at Balleul.	SR
	23/5/17		At rest at ARRAS	

Army Form C. 2118.

WAR DIARY
or
INTELLIGENCE SUMMARY.

(Erase heading not required.) H.Q. 11 K.T.or R.F.A.

May 1917.

Place	Date	Hour	Summary of Events and Information	Remarks and references to Appendices
HAZARCQ	24/5/17		Brigade marched to HAZARCQ. H.Q.s being there for the night with C/71 and D/71. B/71 & B/71 at NOYELLETTE	J.07
ETREE WAMIN	25/5/17		Brigade marched to ETREE WAMIN.	
BOUBERS SUR CANCHE	26/5/17		Brigade marched to BOUBERS sur CANCHE	
"	27/5/17		at BOUBERS sur CANCHE ahead	
"	28/5/17		"	
"	29/5/17		Major General R. P. C. Lecky covering Artillery 5th Army inspected the Brigade at BOUBERS.	
"	30/5/17		at BOUBERS.	
"	31/5/17		at BOUBERS sur CANCHE ahead.	

[signature]
Lt Col
Cmdg 11 R.F.A.
31/5/17

CONFIDENTIAL.

WAR DIARY

of

71st BRIGADE, R.F.A.

From 1st June, 1917. To 30th June 1917.

VOLUME 24

Army Form C. 2118.

WAR DIARY
or
INTELLIGENCE SUMMARY.
(Erase heading not required.)

H.Q. 4.11 "B" R.F.A. VOL 22

June 1917.

Place	Date	Hour	Summary of Events and Information	Remarks and references to Appendices
BOUDERS sur CANCHE	1/6/17		Distribution of Belgian Medals by Major General McCracken commanding 15 Division. Inspection of Officers also carried out by General McCracken as well as by Brigadier General Buchanan Coun "I" 15 G.s.A.	mt
"	2/6/17		at BOUDERS sur CANCHE arrest for having buypoel.	mts
"	3/6/17		"	mts
"	4/6/17		Inspection D.O.D.A. - competitions sec a/Aubromet	mts
"	5/6/17		Vehicles & horses judged by Major General R McLecky.	mts
"	6/6/17		at BOUDERS sur CANCHE arrest - having continued	mts
"	7/6/17		"	mts
"	8/6/17		"	mts
"	9/6/17		"	mts
"	10/6/17		"	mts
"	11/6/17		"	mts
"	12/6/17		"	mts
"	13/6/17		"	mts
"	14/6/17		"	mts
"	15/6/17		"	mts

Army Form C. 2118.

WAR DIARY
or
INTELLIGENCE SUMMARY.
1/1 RB at HQ, R.B.

(Erase heading not required.)

June 1917

Place	Date	Hour	Summary of Events and Information	Remarks and references to Appendices
EPS.	18/6/17		Brigade marched from BOUBERS sur CANCHE to EPS. arriving 12.0 noon	
ST HILAIRE	19/6/17		Brigade marched from EPS to ST HILAIRE. A/71 moving on to NORRENT FONTES. Brigade arrived at 10.0 a.m.	
STEEN BECQUE	18/6/17		Brigade marched from EPS to STEEN BECQUE arriving at 8.0 a.m	
"	19/6/17		At STEEN BECQUE area.	
EECKE	20/6/17		Brigade marched to EECKE. Batteries in MONTEBOSCH area arrived at EECKE at 8.0 a.m.	
WATOU	21/6/17		Brigade marched to WATOU arriving at midnight.	
"	22/6/17		Brigade HQrs moved from farm kurd into WATOU.	
"	23/6/17		At WATOU street.	
"	24/6/17		WATOU street. Advance parties 8 officers + 25 men proceeded to Ney-under Capt Allan. B/71 went up to prepare positions rear YPRES.	
"	25/6/17			
"	26/6/17		At WATOU street	

WAR DIARY or INTELLIGENCE SUMMARY

Army Form C. 2118.

40th & 41st Bde RFA

June 1917

Place	Date	Hour	Summary of Events and Information	Remarks and references to Appendices
WATOU	27/6/17		at WATOU etcat.	600
"	28/6/17		"	
"	29/6/17		"	
"	30/6/17		"	

June 30/17.

[signature]
Comm 41st Bde RFA

CONFIDENTIAL.

WAR DIARY

of

71st Brigade R.F.A.

From 1st October 1917.   To 31st October, 1917.

(Volume 28).

WAR DIARY or INTELLIGENCE SUMMARY

Army Form C. 2118.

HQ II/72 RFA   Oct 1917

Place	Date	Hour	Summary of Events and Information	Remarks and references to Appendices
ATHIES	1/10/17		Our artillery fired at enemy T.M's and M.G's during the day and carried out harassing fire on enemy tracks at night. Hostile artillery shelled CORPS SWITCH NORTH with 4.2's from HOYAN WOOD during the morning. LANCER LINE & SCABBARD ALLEY lightly shelled in the afternoon. E.A. active. Visibility I.C.	[i]
"	2/10/17		Our artillery fired at various M.G's and T.M's mainly at the respective points of activity, and also fired at movement. Hostile artillery shelled our front lightly all the morning. Enemy A.A. guns active. Visibility poor in morning but improved later.	[ii]
"	3/10/17		Our artillery fired at enemy T.M's and also enemy trenches. Hostile artillery fired at intervals on 2ND DON ALLEY - SUNKEN ROAD & HOPI LANCER AVENUE & other trenches but only very few rounds. Hostile artillery aerial activity visibility very poor.	[iii]
"	4/10/17		Our artillery carried out their programme also fired on enemy movement. Hostile artillery very slight activity. Visibility fair in morning but moved in late afternoon.	[iv]

Army Form C. 2118.

WAR DIARY
or
INTELLIGENCE SUMMARY.
(Erase heading not required.)

HQ 4 1 2 a R FA

Oct 1/17

Instructions regarding War Diaries and Intelligence Summaries are contained in F.S. Regs., Part II. and the Staff Manual respectively. Title pages will be prepared in manuscript.

Place	Date	Hour	Summary of Events and Information	Remarks and references to Appendices
ATHIES	5/10/17		Our batteries fired at hostile Trench Mortar emplacements at intervals during the day. Movement was as usual seen and fired on, apparently causing some casualties. During the night enemy tracks and dug-outs were kept under intermittent fire. Throughout the morning enemy lightly shelled our trench system but was very quiet during the afternoon and evening.	PW
	6/10/17		Hostile artillery activity considerably below normal. Visibility was bad & little movement was seen.	PW
	7/10/17		Visibility bad - rain all day. The 11th A.&S.H. raided the enemy's lines supported by a box barrage. A dug-out was bombed and one prisoner, who was killed by a shell whilst being brought in, was captured. The raid took place at 9.15 in very bad weather.	PW
	8/10/17		Usual work seen in Park Work & Regent Trench. When fired on work ceased for about 1 hour, when it was resumed.	PW
	9/10/17		Normal activity - registration of various trenches carried out, in preparation for bombardment of 12th Divisional Front -	PW

T.J134. Wt. W708-776. 500000. 4/15. Sir J. C. & S.

WAR DIARY
or
INTELLIGENCE SUMMARY.
(Erase heading not required.)

Army Form C. 2118.

HQ 1/2 R.F.A.

Oct 17.

Place	Date	Hour	Summary of Events and Information	Remarks and references to Appendices
ATHIES	10.10.17		We fired on T.M's & M.G's and on movement during the day and searched enemy tracks during the night. One E.A was brought down by M.G. fire South of Monchy.	RMS
	11.10.17		Hostile activity normal. We carried out our usual programme.	RMS
	12.10.17		Our 18 prs fired on a working party during the morning causing at least six casualties. T.M's were active against our front line. T.M's were shelled at the infantry's request.	RMS
	13.10.17		We carried out our daily programme - so did the enemy.	RMS
	14.10.17		We fired during the six hours bombardment & raid by the 12th Division, in which they captured 60 prisoners.	HF
	15.10.17		Our artillery fired at enemy T.M's & enemy trenches. Enemy T.M's offensive. Hostile Arty heavy & shelled wd 1 & 3. Visibility 100. Very artillery fired at movement & several T.M's. Enemy T.M's	OF
	16.10.17		active on our front line. Visibility fair.	HF
	17.10.17		We fired on movement during the day, & searched tracks, trenches as usual night. Stalinth hostile shelling there was nearly on the front line system. Visibility fair.	HF

WAR DIARY
or
INTELLIGENCE SUMMARY.

Army Form C. 2118.

October 1917

Place	Date	Hour	Summary of Events and Information	Remarks and references to Appendices
Map Ref 14 E.2	18/10/17		Our artillery fired early at TM's. Hostile artillery much below normal. We fired as usual on TM's & back at enemy. Hostile artillery below normal.	
"	19/10/17		Our artillery fired at enemy strong point & also at OPs. Wire cutting. Hostile artillery below normal.	
"	20/10/17			
"	21/10/17		Our artillery fired on movement at various times during the day. At 5.30 pm we fired on SOS MAND — something to stop an enemy raid. Opened fire at 6.0 pm. Hostile artillery below normal. Visibility poor. Very little enemy activity.	
"	22/10/17		Our artillery fired reading programme. Hostile artillery very quiet. Personal EA activity. Visibility poor.	
"	23/10/17		Our artillery carried out their usual programme & fired on enemy TM's in retaliation for hostile shelling. Hostile artillery quiet. Opposite us in LANCER AVENUE during the afternoon. Visibility poor.	
"	24/10/17		Our artillery carried out a bombardment round a road made by 61 Bde on our left at 12.30. TM's again in the afternoon. Also judged enemy working parties. Hostile reply to our bombardment was not very heavy. Light calibre wired LANCER LANE were shelled somewhat during the evening till 4.0.	

WAR DIARY or INTELLIGENCE SUMMARY

Army Form C. 2118.

October 1917

Place	Date	Hour	Summary of Events and Information	Remarks and references to Appendices
ATHIES	24/10/17		Our artillery carried out a bombardment of POWDER TRENCH and also dispersed enemy working parties. A few enemy shells (4.2) fell in & MONCHY. Hostile artillery below normal. Visibility good in morning only	
	26/10/17		Our artillery engaged several T.M. positions. Akrugel fired on Sunday Rock. D/H fired 100 chemical shell at dugouts in I.13.6 to 25. Enemy fired about 30 rounds 4.2 at ORANGE HILL during the morning. Afternoon dud. Visibility bad	
	27/4/17		Our artillery fired at various positions & attempted on tracks & harassed hostile artillery fire. A few rounds 77mm in LANCER AVENUE in morning. 4.2 rounds E.A. activity Hostile slight.	
	28/10/17		Our artillery fired at MONK TRENCH & several T.M.s Hostile artillery fired 30 rounds 8" in I.19.c. from clutches of JIGSAW WOOD in the morning. E.A.activity Visibility P.O. Shs relieved by A/40.	
"	29/10/17		Our artillery fired at MONK TRENCH & CIGAR C.P.16 during the day. Also dispersed several working parties. Hostile artillery shelled HOST from I.11.24.90	

Army Form C. 2118.

WAR DIARY
or
INTELLIGENCE SUMMARY.
(Erase heading not required.)

October 1917.   HQ 41st B.D. R.F.A.

Instructions regarding War Diaries and Intelligence Summaries are contained in F. S. Regs., Part II. and the Staff Manual respectively. Title pages will be prepared in manuscript.

Place	Date	Hour	Summary of Events and Information	Remarks and references to Appendices
ATH/1ST	28/10/17 (cont)		About 50 rounds H.E. were fired in retaliation on HAT TRENCH & A action in afternoon. Visibility poor - nothing seen.	
"	29/10/17		Our artillery retaliated on various T.M's at request of the infantry both by day & night. Attempt refused on taction J.52 & J.14 on account of suspected enemy relief. Hostile artillery very active throughout the day on H3 & C4 and K21 & S21. Guns ceasing about 8.30 pm. Otherwise a quiet day. Visibility good in morning - bad in afternoon.	
	30/10/17		Our artillery carried out their bombardment programme & fired in sundry T.M.C. SO.S. artillery normal. Visibility bad, rain pouring.	
	31/10/17			

W. Wynne Lieut Col
Comdg 41st Bde R.F.A.

CONFIDENTIAL.

WAR DIARY

of

71st Brigade R.F.A.

(Volume 28)

From 1st November 1917.   To 30th November 1917.

WAR DIARY or INTELLIGENCE SUMMARY

Army Form C. 2118.

HQ 71-73rd RFA

November 1917

Vol 27

Place	Date	Hour	Summary of Events and Information	Remarks and references to Appendices
ATHIES	Nov 1/17		Our artillery fired at enemy TM's during the day, also at movement in various places, especially PARK WORK. Hostile artillery fired in the morning rather more actively in the afternoon. Enemy TM's ORANGE AVENUE & MONCHY shelled at intervals. F.A. No action taken in result.	
	Nov 2/17		Usual retaliation on enemy T.M.s with good results. New enemy trench heavily shelled with 4.5 & considerable damage caused. During the night tracks in enemy back area received sporadic attention, and dug outs were attacked with chemical shell at 12.50.	C/A/1 2.17
			Hostile artillery lightly shelled our front line & 4.2's fired on our support trenches. Visibility poor: movement seen about VICTORIA COPSE.	
	Nov 3/17		Day quiet visibility bad.	C/A/2
	Nov 4/17		Enemy heavily barraged division on our right with guns, how. & TM's of all calibres. Rt. Bn. of our Bn. Bde. received fringes of this. Fire lasted from 1.35 am to 2.5 am. In response to S.O.S. call we fired from 1.50 am to 2.10 am, 700 rounds being expended.	C/A/3

Army Form C. 2118.

WAR DIARY
or
INTELLIGENCE SUMMARY.
(Erase heading not required.)

November 1917   H.Q. 71st Bde. R.F.A.

Place	Date	Hour	Summary of Events and Information	Remarks and references to Appendices
ATHIES	Nov 4/17		Rest of day quiet until 4.30 pm when we harrased enemy along points by way of diverting his attention from aerial photo work : enemy replied after 9 minutes but his harrase was then scattered. This firing ceased at 5.30. Enemy T.M.'s shelled as usual. Hostile guns quiet : T.M.'s active. There were dealt with : observation being almost impossible tracks in snow, tracks back area were kept under intermittent fire, during the day part of the night. A working party at PARK WOOD was dispersed by our fire at 3.30 pm.	C/M
	Nov 5/17		Enemy artillery quiet. Movement seen & engaged in POODLE & TREE trenches. Chemical shells bombardment took place on enemy dugouts in I.I is a at 11.15 pm this recent. was subsequently swept by shrapnel. Enemy artillery quite active. I.31.a received attention from 77 mm from direction of jigsaw wood between 10.30 am & 12 noon. An hour later 4.25 dropped 30 rds on I.31.d from direction of QUARRY WOOD. Between 4.20 pm 16.10 pm some 300-5.9's fell in H.34 r another 50 rds between 6 & 8.30 pm this probably in reply to wirecutting along DEVIL'S TRENCH from this sector.	C/M
	Nov 6/17			C/M
	Nov 7/17			C/M

Army Form C. 2118.

WAR DIARY
or
INTELLIGENCE SUMMARY.
(Erase heading not required.)

H.Q. 71st Bde. R.F.A.

November 1917

Place	Date	Hour	Summary of Events and Information	Remarks and references to Appendices
ATHIES	Nov 7/17 (Contd)		In response to 77mm on our Suffolk Enemy TM's received retaliation at 10.30am. POWDER TRENCH was also engaged by 18pdrs. FACTION TRENCH received 100 rds 4.5 at 12.30. 20 rounds 4.5 – 106 fuze were fired at Enemy wire & good results obtained. TM's were engaged in O3a, O2c, I33c at request of Infantry. Considerable movement seen in JIGSAW WOOD. Camouflage has been erected at hut Southerly corner. Visibility poor to fair.	C/SM
	Nov 8/17		Enemy lightly shelled our front lines supports with 77mm & a few 4.2's. He retaliated on other line & on working parties. Visibility poor to fair, later on poor.	C/SM
	Nov 9/17		A party of the KOSB left our lines at 1.40 am with the intention of entering DEVILS trench but found pit in Enemy wire too strongly held. Our TM's active during the night but hostile artillery were less active than usual.	C/SM
	Nov 10/17		Enemy sent over a few TM bombs during the day & between 2.45 pm & 4.15 pm. Some 30 - 5.9's fell on LAURA TRENCH. Director JIGSAW WOOD. We retaliated on TM's during day, and engaged what little movement was seen. Night quiet. Visibility fair to poor.	C/SM
	Nov 11/17		Few S.9's fell on FAMPOUX in the morning: about 100 4.2 airbursts over	C/SM

WAR DIARY or INTELLIGENCE SUMMARY

Army Form C. 2118.

HQ 71st Bde R.F.A.

Nov 1917

Place	Date	Hour	Summary of Events and Information	Remarks and references to Appendices
ATHIES	Nov 11/17 (Contd)		1 one H.22 1/4 23. No damage. SCABBARD TRENCH shelled by TM's in front line enemy's MG emplacements. Small amt of TM ammunition sent up at T.26.c.3.5.6.0. One AA aeroplane over lines at 11hr was driven off by AA.	C/71A
	Nov 12/17		From 3.15 am to 4.30 am H.22 & H.27d were shelled by gas shell & 4.2 H.E. Damage negligable. JOHNSON AVENUE received a few 77mm in the afternoon.	C/71A
		At 10 pm POWDER TRENCH was bombarded by 10/pdrs. 450 rds being used. 150 were cutting rounds were fired at T.31.G.9050. Enemy aircraft active over our lines during afternoon.	150 C/71A
	Nov 13/17		Enemy artillery inactive. We lightly shelled his back areas. TM's but observed shoots were impossible. The 70th Bde R.F.A. pulled out their guns & left section of C/71 came up from 3rd Army Artillery school, & took over C/70's position, borrowing a section from A/71. Major Graham DSO MC in command A/307 (61st Div.) took over C/70's position & are lent to 15th DA for S.O.S. purpose.	C/71A
	Nov 14/17		Enemy Artillery very quiet. Ours also, about 100 rounds being expended on TM emplac-	C/71A

Army Form C. 2118.

WAR DIARY
or
INTELLIGENCE SUMMARY.
(Erase heading not required.)

HQ 71st Bde RFA

Nov. 1917

Instructions regarding War Diaries and Intelligence Summaries are contained in F.S. Regs., Part II. and the Staff Manual respectively. Title pages will be prepared in manuscript.

Place	Date	Hour	Summary of Events and Information	Remarks and references to Appendices
ATHIES.	Nov 14 (contd)		Tracks in I.26c or I.25 or tracks in I.33c. Visibility poor to nil	
	Nov 15/17.		The enemys artillery showed little activity. A few Minen fell in MONCHY, ROEUX the firing place received 8 rounds from 4.2's. LANCER AVENUE also came under fire from 4.2's & 4 medium TM bombs fell at H.25c76.	C of A
		At 11 a.m.	6" Hows effectively shelled GRENADE TRENCH but no movement was seen; the hostile TM's at 2.30 p.m. whilst it was in progress own heavy TM's dropped 50 rounds on POWDER TRENCH; wire was also cut in the TM's at I.31a.40.35; about I.32a.00.30. Between 3 v.t in the afternoon 15pdrs cut wire at I.31a.40.35; about 100 rounds. This bombardment caused a fire in enemy lines which burnt to about ½h. late fires were observed firing in PLOUVAIN y were engaged. At 4.30 we fired in support of raid by 183W Inf Bde 61st Div on our left. Tracks fired on as usual during the night. Medium TM's fired on own front line in I.25.c & A.2's in I.25d, probably retaliatory shelling.	
	Nov 16/17		At 2 a.m we fired in support of raid by Division on our right. At 11 a.m. we dealt with TM's in I.32.b & c. ANGEL & DEVIL TRENCH PELVES roads in I.25d were shelled by own TM's & DEVIL FACTION CARTRIDGE POWDER by 18pdrs. 6" hows wire was cut at	C of A

WAR DIARY or INTELLIGENCE SUMMARY

Army Form C. 2118.

HQ. 71st Bde. R.F.A   Nov. 1917

Place	Date	Hour	Summary of Events and Information	Remarks and references to Appendices
ATHIES	Nov 14/17		T.31.d.90.80. Tracks engaged Co roads during the night. Two E.A's were seen driven off by M.A.	C/M
	Nov 15/17		Hostile artillery very quiet. SCABBARD SUPPORT, ROFUX & LANCER AVENUE were all shelled lightly with 4.2's direction JIGSAW WOOD. Aitherets A.2 are ATHIES & FAMPOUX. At 4.30 am we barraged in support of raid by 8th Seaforth Highlanders who entered the enemy trench killed one man. Enemy TM's were dealt with during the day in T.26.c. CORN TRENCH was bombarded by others & movement in HAT TRENCH successfully engaged. At 6.30 pm we fired in support of raid by 11th A.V.H. & again at 7.15 pm to aid 4th Div on our right. Targets in T.27.a.1. T.31.l. T.33.a. T.27t were engaged during the night.	C/J/o
	Nov 16/17		From 12 noon to 12.36 77mm shells were twenty rounds A.2. dropped in T.25.c during course of afternoon our front line was being heavy N & usu. HAPPY VALLEY also received 4,000 dead Hallientin. Fire was also heavy late on upon the right battalion Howl left brigade. JOHNSON AVENUE also came in for trench SO S.9 & A.2. In return to our barrage at 6 pm the enemy opened up their barrage at 6.10 pm 77th shrapnel chiefly. Our winds left barrage	C/J/o

Army Form C. 2118.

WAR DIARY
or
INTELLIGENCE SUMMARY.
(Erase heading not required.)

HQ. 71st Bde. R.F.A.

Nov. 1917

Place	Date	Hour	Summary of Events and Information	Remarks and references to Appendices
ATHIES	Nov 18/17	(contd)	Nickname 4.2's taking part. This fell on our front Suffolk communication trenches in T.25, T.31. Our batteries engaged a fair amount of movement in enemy back areas; no round per was spent on enemy batteries active in PLOUVAIN. Gun flash was considerably damaged by 200 rounds from our 4.5 hows. One such TM was silenced. At 6 p.m. we fired in support of raid by the 13th Royal Scots and kept the usual tasks under fire all night.	
	Nov 19/17		Hostile Artillery showed fair interest in life & fired intermittently with TMs & 4.2's upon H.29, T.25. This sporadic fire became a barrage at 1.55 p.m. & on trenches were thoroughly searched. Enemy's barrage in reply to ours at 7.15 p.m. was thin & weak, but apparently in the right place, chiefly T.25, A.27. A.E.L.I French received a good deal of fire from us during the day & many casualties were caused. At 12 noon, we bombarded GREENLAND HILL movement was engaged & wire cut at T.31.6.97. TM's engaged as usual. At 7.15 p.m. a raid was carried out by 13th Royal Scots who met	

WAR DIARY or INTELLIGENCE SUMMARY

Army Form C. 2118.

HQ 7th Bde R.F.A.

Nov 1917

Place	Date	Hour	Summary of Events and Information	Remarks and references to Appendices
ATHIES.	Nov 19 (cont.)		with little success. At 11pm to 4.5 hows fired 100 P.S. h aid raid by 61st Div.	C/M
	Nov 20/17		At 6.30 am we fired in support of raid by 4th Div. Previous to this carried out a gas bombardment with 4.5 hows during which B171 fired 300 Coronial rounds. After amount of retirement usual gas and engaged. Small losses were inflicted upon the enemy. During the night some 400 rounds were spent in harassing tasks. At 11.50 am again at 3pm the enemy put over some 30 5.9s and seven 4.2s upon H22. Late on SCABBARD ALLEY, JOHNSON AVENUE V/A HAPPY VALLEY area were retaliated with 5.9's 4.2s & 77mm.	C/M
	Nov 21/17		The enemy's retaliation to our morning raid was much thin: it opened 15' after our zero hour & was scattered. He had suffered this chiefly 4.2s. During his worrying his T.M's were busy. He cut some of our wire near Y sap. We carried out a rifle raid at 6 am by Royal Scots, Camerons & H.L.I. R.S. penetrated enemy front line & found 2 large dugouts held strongly by oblique M.G fire the 10th H.L.I found them detective & were bombed back. T.M's were silenced during the day & destruction they reports our barrage good.	C/M

WAR DIARY
or
INTELLIGENCE SUMMARY.
(Erase heading not required.)

H.Q. 71st Bde R.F.A.

Nov 1917

Army Form C. 2118.

Place	Date	Hour	Summary of Events and Information	Remarks and references to Appendices
ATHIES	Nov 21/17 (C.A.)		fire directed upon BELT, FUZE, CARAVAN trench. At 10.5 pm acting enemy patrol approached the cut wire at Y but retired when off by a steady concentration already arranged for this contingency. Altho' we fired in support of raid by 184th Bde. During this day the hostiles were on the qui vive & prepared to advance in event of Enemy withdrawal.	C.A/n
	Nov 22/17		Enemy again tried to cut our wire at T.25.d.3.0. with T.M's. Also with 4.2's. ORANGE AVENUE RESERVE were raked by 77mm. Had Suffolk him with rifle SCARPE were heavily shelled from QUARRY WOOD area by 4.2's. Concentrated shorts were also carried out on the same calibre at T.31.c.r.d. T.25.c.v.d. T.31.a.1. direction as before Enchelart. Overseas about 30'. O.1.a. also shared the general unpopularity. On 19 pdrs cut wire along Sunny hort. Some 1900 rounds being used, several retn. made. T.M's were silenced. Y CARTRIDGE trench received attention also, PELVES, JIGSAW WOOD, CHAMBRAIN ROAD T.33.a.1. were dealt with during the night.	C.A/n
	Nov 23/17	11.41.3 pm	ROEUX etc. shelled heavily by S.G.'s 4.2's between 9/10 between on T.31.c.v.d. received the same treatment from 4.2's & 77 mm	C.A/n

WAR DIARY
or
INTELLIGENCE SUMMARY.

Army Form C. 2118.

Nov. 1917 H.Q. 71st Bde R.F.A.

Place	Date	Hour	Summary of Events and Information	Remarks and references to Appendices
ATHIES	Nov 3/11/17	(contd.)	Heavy TM's & a few S.O.S. also contributed. Fire chiefly from BOIRY HAMBLAIN. Guns 2 to 2.20 p.m. A concentration of 77mm HA's was put down on our front support lines in I 31 a.b. Hostile artillery activity aggressive on this day.	
			We shelled in the day chiefly in cutting wire in I 31 c. with 18 pdr. 50 rounds BX 106 fuze was also employed. Damage to wire considerable. 32 T.M's were also silenced. During the night JIGSAW WOOD BEEHYTREE trenches & enemy lights were searched by 200 rds 18 pdr.	Copy.
			Visibility pres. a.m. fair for	
	Nov 4/11/17		Hostile guns active in the morning, but the batteries opp. ourselves area. At 2.30 p.m. fire was concentrated on front support lines in I 30 C 31. 4.2's being the worst offenders. This lasted for 15 minutes. At 3.40 ROEUX VON BOCK line in I 20 a were headed in a similar manner.	Copy.
			Heavy TMs also took part. In the morning we silenced a few TMs & engaged movement whenever seen: ANGEL DEVIL ARCHIE APE trenches were heavily shelled by 18 pdrs. A SO was being used.	

Army Form C. 2118.

WAR DIARY
or
INTELLIGENCE SUMMARY.
(Erase heading not required.) H.Q. 71st Bde R.F.A.

November 1917

Place	Date	Hour	Summary of Events and Information	Remarks and references to Appendices
ATHIES	Nov 24/17 (cont)	4.5 hours	dealt with POWDER MONK GRENADE FACTION. At 4.20 p.m. the French bombardment was repeated. At night we spent 500 rds 18pdr. & 75 Rx on enemy cross roads, dugouts, track trenches & railways.	a/s
	Nov 25/17		At 7.30 Hostile A.2s & 5.9s shelled ROEUX fairly heavily but fire after this was somewhat desultory until 1.20 when some 100 4.2s searched H 29.d, & about 60 5.9s H 29.c. direction JIGSAW WOOD. Shelling after this was casual. At 11.30 r.7p.m. 150 18pdrs shells were directed at FRICTION, & 100 Rx spent to good purpose in CARTRIDGE French. The junction of CARROT & CARAVAN was also searches up & down how an 18pdr battery successfully CARAVAN altho' same time. Movement this expert to wound. 200 rounds 18pdr was spent all night on enemy backarea. Considerable movement was seen in the SAILLY-VITRY road moving both north & south. This was thought to be the relief of the corps heavier but effect was not seen.	a/s

WAR DIARY
INTELLIGENCE SUMMARY

HQ 11 VB CRFA

Nov 1914

Place	Date	Hour	Summary of Events and Information	Remarks and references to Appendices
ATHIES	Nov 26/14		Hostile artillery obstinate. A number of heavy TMs fell in front the system during the day. Our artillery fired obstinately with some success and also retaliated on hostile TMs. Hostile aircraft crossed our lines several times. Visibility poor on an - horizon.	WD
"	Nov 27/14		Hostile artillery shelled BROWNY TRIANGLE at intervals with a 9"or 5gun. Afterwards during the day - offensive comparing inactive. Our artillery fired on enemy trench system with good results. Visibility fair.	WD
"	Nov 28/14		Shelling of RAILWAY TRIANGLE continued. Orilla shelling of MONCHY mainly 4.2" from S to SW. ORANGE HILL also shelled with 4.2"c. OU engaged a considerable number of TMs. One 6"D captured a reconnaissance of our lines. Visibility poor but improving.	WD
FEUCHY	Nov 29/14		BHQ moved at 11.0 am to H23 c 5.90. A141. C141 + D141 came under control of 61"SA. Losing a group with B/207. A141 wait with the control of 6.1"DA. 13 Siege Buyde 61"SA at 12 noon of 61"DA. Find and landed over R12 4 Jan 16 6 0 BTY. H524	WD

WAR DIARY
or
INTELLIGENCE SUMMARY.

Army Form C. 2118.

HQ 11 12 A RFA

Nov 1917.

Place	Date	Hour	Summary of Events and Information	Remarks and references to Appendices
FEUCHY Jan 29th Cont'd H.22c50.50.			Artillery reported in action on H.21 a+c sh 51c+ 53d. Barrage put up by Enemy M.G. very broken away. Our line carried out a chemical bombardment in early morning. Our reply arrived in a very slight bombardment at 2.0pm.	Ap 9.
"	Jan 30/17		Hostile artillery comparatively inactive in early morning. Our artillery did no shooting up to 4.0am. Enemy does hostile artillery activity increased considerably later in the morning.	Ap 9.

Signed /s/ [signature]
Com. OIC 12 A RFA
30/1/17

CONFIDENTIAL.

WAR DIARY

of

71st Brigade R.F.A.

(Volume 29).

From 1st December 1917.   to 31st December 1917.

Army Form C. 2118.

WAR DIARY
or
INTELLIGENCE SUMMARY.
(Erase heading not required.)

HQ 71ᵗʰ Bᵈᵉ RFA

December 1917

VM 28

Place	Date	Hour	Summary of Events and Information	Remarks and references to Appendices
FAMPOUX H23 c 50 90	30/11/17		Hostile artillery quiet on our front. Monday heavy shells by 4" guns between 10.0 & 10.10 am from direction of QUARRY WOOD and again later in the morning at 5.9's. Our artillery fired at movement of 50 men in HATCHET WOOD at 4.45 pm and retaliated on TM's. A.A.M.G. other movement seen. E.A. activity nil.	D.V
	1/12/17		Hostile artillery (4.2's and 5.9's) active intermittently throughout the day on H 22 B & H 23 C. Our artillery carried out their programme of shoots including back & roads at night. Low E.A. activity. Visibility good.	D.V
	2/12/17		Hostile artillery again shelled H 23 C and FAMPOUX x-roads, also x-roads throughout the day. MON CITY & LONE COPSE also received some attention. Fired on movement at various times and carried out their allotted tasks. Many enemy planes about.	D.V
	4/12/17		Great E.A. activity vicinity gap. Hostile artillery less active during the day but more so at night. H 23 c & 22 a received a considerable amount of H.E gas and H.E.	D.V

Army Form C. 2118.

WAR DIARY
or
INTELLIGENCE SUMMARY.
(Erase heading not required.)

Nov. 1917.   HQ 172nd R.F.A.

Place	Date	Hour	Summary of Events and Information	Remarks and references to Appendices
FAMPOUX	4/11/17	(cont'd)	Our artillery carried out various shoots on enemy trenches during the day, and also retaliated for 4.2's on BITCHE. Saw retaliation also on hostile TMs. Charges fired on road & track. E.A. active. Visibility poor in morning, interrupted later.	App
"	5/11/17		Hostile artillery moderately quiet. H.4.9 to 10.30 a.m. some little attention on K22 & S.19 Sect. intervals. Our artillery fired several shoots working parties and D/11 carried out a successful registration shoot on I.11.c.5.2 in the morning. LFA swept from one or two likely several patterns up during the day. Visibility good.	App
"	6/11/17		Hostile artillery rather more active. About 150 rounds 4.2 fired into H22a during the day. Our careful registration by means of an aeroplane from H ruined in J VIT.RY. Shells came from the direction of VITRY. Saw TM activity also. Our artillery carried out various shoots including on CAPSTAN TRENCH. At 2.15pm we fired on SOS signal W. inspired by the infantry, EA artillery active. Visibility poor, except H22 being the chief objects.	App
"	7/11/17		Hostile artillery about normal, chiefly with 4.2's. Our artillery carried on a succession of retaliatory shoots on TM's & usual strafes fired on tracks and enemy work.	App

WAR DIARY or INTELLIGENCE SUMMARY.

Army Form C. 2118.

HQ. 1st "Z" A.R.A.

Dec/1917.

Place	Date	Hour	Summary of Events and Information	Remarks and references to Appendices
FAMPOUX	9/12/17		Hostile artillery was well distributed over the whole sector, including a few rounds into ROEUX & MONCHY at 4.20 p.m. the enemy put down a barrage of all calibres up to 5.9" including whizz bell on the PECKET sector. This O.G. lasted about 10 minutes. Our artillery fired at movement and various T.M's. At 4.10 all batteries fired 2½ minutes S.O.S. slow rate on Salut W. Several enemy of batter spotted during the day. E.A. above normal. Visibility poor to fair.	A.D
"	10/12/17		Hostile artillery slightly active, mainly on H.16 b.c. & H.11 c. tranches, 4.2's, 5.9ins & rockets. We carried out destruction shoots upon CANDY & CLIFF trenches and retaliation on various T.M's. Visibility for E.A. nil.	A.D
"	11/12/17		A few rounds fell into MONCHY and ROEUX HQ V.C and HQ C. were heavily shelled during the morning also H.29 at in the afternoon. A barrage was put down on our front as tapping in times S of the COSTE for 4.50 to 5.15 p.m. Our artillery fired 20 rounds into COD & Farm 6.59. Isolated C.B.M. reached 800 rounds and Engaged in infantry request. Aerial ranging by 5.15 pm Junction Switch W. sur Fauboy registered. E.A. very active in morning. Visibility fair.	A.D
"	12/12/17		Hostile fire considerably below normal. Consisting mainly of 4.2's and Whizz bangs in MONCHY. Our artillery engaged a certain amount of movement 5.9's into MONCHY retaliated on T.M's and straight fire on tracks & road. Visibility poor.	A.D

WAR DIARY or INTELLIGENCE SUMMARY

Army Form C. 2118.

Place: FAMPOUX
Date: Dec 1917
Unit: HQ 41" [?]ZD RFA

Date	Hour	Summary of Events and Information	Remarks and references to Appendices
17/12/17		Hostile artillery exhibited its fairness being rather quiet over the area to-day. Day average being registered 50-60 rounds. 4.2" on E.2.a from Vitasse. HV etc.m. minor. Very slow. Mostly in the evening. We carried out our programme shoot which included a gas bombardment on PELVES LANE POWDER & other trenches. Gas was exchanged at 8.10 p.m. & our fire opened the discharge. Enemy replied at 8.10 p.m. with a slight fire, [?] our lines. E.A. about normal. Visibility poor.	DDD
18/12/17		Hostile artillery below normal. Our artillery carried out their programme at 12 noon. The group came under a H/F 15 DA and included A/141, B/141, C/141, D/141 & C/215. A/50 returned to B & DA group. Visibility poor.	DD
19/12/17		Hostile artillery was active a little shelling of LANCER LANE with 77mm H.E. in the morning. 4.2.5pm a very heavy barrage of all calibres was opened on our front line between the new & railway as well as TM's 426a - 426a. 426a & 426b were also [?] ceased at 2.15 pm. LANCER LONG - 426a. 426b were also shelled afterwards during the afternoon. Our artillery fired 200 rounds repel CEOD & CAP STAN at 1.30 p.m. & 2.5 p.m. in response to SOS signals. Fired on normal [?] [?] at 2.10 p.m. this was acked to K5/03 CRUST. Opened firing at 2 & 6 p.m. 3.0 p.m. DTM fired 100 rounds at the junction of [?] & ELOD Sunday. TM's were silenced during the day. No EA activity. Visibility poor. C/215	DD

(A7032). Wt. W13539/M1393. 75,000. 1/17. D. D. & L., Ltd. Forms/C2118/44.

WAR DIARY or INTELLIGENCE SUMMARY

Army Form C. 2118.

9.10.1917   HQ 71 "B" Coy RFA

Place	Date	Hour	Summary of Events and Information	Remarks and references to Appendices
FAMPOUX	15/10/17		Hostile artillery was not particularly active, although there was a certain amount of T.M. hostility. Our artillery carried out systematic shoot on sundry shoulders & fired at T.M's harassment. Visibility fair to indifferent. EA very active in the morning.	OP
"	16/10/17		Hostile artillery activity abnormal. Our artillery fired at several harassment & T.M's in response to registration. EA and visibility poor. The remaining personnel of Sgt Coy up at active positions. C/59 moved from HAUTE-CLOQUE. 2 guns sent back to reparation & repaired.	OP
"	17/10/17		Hostile artillery again quiet only indulging in very occasional small shoots. Our artillery performed a few worthy shoots. Several T.M's & fired at usual areas & night. EA and visibility poor.	OP
"	18/10/17		Hostile artillery showed a little more activity. Between 2 & 6 x 3.9 50 rounds 4.2 were fired at H.3.d from B.O.1.R.7 and at 4.0 A.M 50 rounds with H.3.c from I.22. At 9.10 P.M. a T.M. barrage in J.14 x 8.c. with T/14. Cal. bracket with 4.2 Our artillery fired at movement and T.M's & T.M. barrage firing. Help of the 3 F.S.C. Canal bridges firing.	OP
"	19/10/17		Hostile artillery active on our left in the early morning. OC & O. area barrage was sent down. All clear by 5.0 a.m. (cont'd)	OP

WAR DIARY or INTELLIGENCE SUMMARY

Army Form C. 2118.

Oct 1917.   HQ 11 r² R.F.A.

Place	Date	Hour	Summary of Events and Information	Remarks and references to Appendices
BEAUMOUX	18/10/17 (cont)		During the day there was hostile enemy activity. After 21 am wd fired on "APR 67" WPR 7 after standing by for some time. At 9.12 we fired on ACI67 RAILWAY as a SOS by our infantry. We fired on ACI67 RAILWAY as a SOS by our infantry. Later in the day we fired at a new enemy trench as well as enemy batteries. Apr firing programme carried out. CFF complete. Then were temporarily in the trenches. Slight EA activity. Visibility poor.	S.R.
"	20/10/17		Hostile artillery fired very little activity. Often TM's firing in the enemy artillery carried out several small bombardments. Our artillery carried out an increased amount owing to the very thick morning. Our artillery natural fire was impressed owing to the very thick by day & night. EA nil.	S.R.
"	21/10/17		Hostile artillery rather more energetic than in the day. After 20 pm a barrage of all calibres including TM's was put down on our front line between TRONCHY and the SCARPE. All quiet by 5.40 pm. TM's and from 5.45 - 6.50 pm our artillery fired at several areas. Normal night firing. EA nil. Visibility nil. Fired on ACIST ANGEL.	S.R.
"	22/10/17		Hostile artillery abnormal. About 5.9's on RSEX in the morning. 4.2's thought to be seen coming in I.3.6. Considerable TM activity. About 300 rounds 5.9 fell in H.2.Y.d during the morning. Our artillery fired on ACI67 CRUST ANDOG on programme of our artillery. Our artillery fired on ACI67 CRUST activity. Visibility poor.	S.R.

WAR DIARY or INTELLIGENCE SUMMARY

Army Form C. 2118.

HQ 41st Bde R.F.A.

December 1917.

Place	Date	Hour	Summary of Events and Information	Remarks and references to Appendices
FAMPOUX	23/12/17		Hostile artillery moderately active during the day. Shots at 6.20 pm a heavy T.M. bombardment on our front line between the river & MONCHY. All calibres found in this H.E. M.G's. Shooting on our rear areas aligned by 7.7 pm. Enemy action took place on our Brit front. Our artillery co-operated being with Slowing Tk's active & day. At 6.57 pm we fired on POSTE ANGER and at 6.32 in response to SOS rockets on Catching Valley fired on "PHILMY's" Our fire slackened at 8.5 pm ceasing at 9.15 pm. Wind: nil. Weather: fine.	OPP
"	24/12/17		At 11.15 ETA activity. Visibility poor. Our artillery carried out 100 harassing fire. Hostile fire reported. ETA activity. Visibility fair. No ho his fire reported by day or night.	OPP
"	25/12/17		Hostile artillery fairly quiet on our front, movement was engaged in back areas during the morning and at 11 a.m. 4.50 rounds were fired on enemy trenches. The usual harassing fire was carried out during the night. Visibility fair.	J
"	26/12/17		Enemy trench mortars were fairly active throughout the day. Hostile artillery and T.M.'s showed slightly increased activity. Our Artillery engaged movements, hostile T.M.'s and during the night various targets in enemy back areas. Shots were seen or first heard of 87° from H.30.c.07.70. Some movement observed on SAILLY-NOYELLES Rd.	J

WAR DIARY
or
INTELLIGENCE SUMMARY.
(Erase heading not required.)

Army Form C. 2118.

Place	Date	Hour	Summary of Events and Information	Remarks and references to Appendices
h) AMPOUX H23C 3090	27/12/17		Visibility poor and occasional breaks. E.A. more active than usual. Hostile artillery somewhat more energetic. We engaged prominent during the day and bombarded a new trench I26a 1842. Between S.12 and S.12 we fired on ASSISTANCE at the request of infantry. We carried out the usual night firing.	J.L.
"	28/12/17		Visibility low to fair. E.A. more active over back areas. Hostile artillery had a fairly busy day and special attention was paid to H13 b.c. and d. 300 4.2 shells fell there between 11-15 and 1-30. No damage. Our artillery bombarded CANDY CORN and CYRIL trenches during the evening and harassed back areas during the night.	J.L.
"	29/12/17		Low visibility low all day. Hostile artillery exceptionally quiet. We bombarded CLIFF during the day with 100 18× and 100 18pdr. The usual night firing was carried out. E.A. were active over back areas during the day.	J.L.
"	30/12/17		Visibility poor. Enemy guns were silent. Minnies 12 and 13 exhibited signs of activity occasionally during the day, but artillery silenced Minnies 12 and 13 and shellie employment at 1.15 P 1540 during the night. Fired on various targets on back areas.	J.L.
"	31/12/17		Visibility poor to fair. Hostile artillery moderately active during the day ROEUX and I.19C receiving most attention. Minnies 1, 12 and 13 showed signs of activity and were silenced. We also bombarded FIG and FOSSIL trenches and observed a working party at H12 & 61. No night firing took place.	J.L.

Signed /s/ Lt Col
Army 7.1.18. 8pm 18.29

CONFIDENTIAL.

WAR DIARY

of

71st Brigade R.F.A.

(Volume 30)

From 1st January 1918   To 31st January 1918.

WAR DIARY
or
INTELLIGENCE SUMMARY

Army Form C. 2118.

Vol 27

Place	Date	Hour	Summary of Events and Information	Remarks and references to Appendices
Fr. FAMPOUX	1/11/18		Visibility fair to good. E.A. were active, one enemy machine was brought down in FAMPOUX at 11-30 a.m. Enemy Artillery was comparatively quiet. We engaged trenches 1·3 and 1,2 and 3 and between 6 h.m. and 10 h.m. fired on CLOD and CAPSTAN and junction of the ROEUX—PLOUVAIN Rd. Lt Col C.M. INGHAM D.S.O. R.F.A. proceeded to D.A. in the absence of the O.C.R.A., Maj F. GRAHAM D.S.O. M.C. R.F.A., C/O. Assumed command of 71st Bde.	JC
	2/11/18		Visibility poor to bad. Enemy seem very quiet. His artillery dispersed movement in CARROT but otherwise did not fire.	JC
	3/11/18		Visibility good. Enemy aerial activity above normal. H22 and H23 were shelled between 9 and 3·30 with 300 5·9 and 8 inch. No damage was done. There was a little other hostile shelling. Gun flashes were observed from H30c 0770 on grid bearings 90°0′ 51 & 55°.	JC
	4/11/18		71st Brigade relieved by 75th & 15th R.F.A. Canvas Division. Guns left in situ.	
ARRAS	5/11/18		Brigade in rest in ARRAS. Drawing ammunition and work on dugouts at Observation position.	
"	6/11/18		D.O.	
"	7/11/18		D.O.	
"	8/11/18		Work of erecting "Willis" pits commenced at observation position.	

WAR DIARY
or
INTELLIGENCE SUMMARY.

(Erase heading not required.)

Army Form C. 2118.

Place	Date	Hour	Summary of Events and Information	Remarks and references to Appendices
ARRAS	9/11/18		Training carried out and work on Observation Position. Dugouts	
"	10/11/18		Do	
"	11/11/18		Training carried out and work commenced on gun pits at Observation Position. In night 11/12" 17 a/s 18s pits were erected on Position, Observation and 12 guns in action	
"	12/11/18		Training carried out and work on Observation Position carried on	
"	13/11/18		Do	
"	14/11/18		Training carried out and work on Observation Position. A/s 18s pits erected	
"	15/11/18		Training carried out and work on Observation and forward Positions	
"	16/11/18		Do	
"	17/11/18		Do	
"	18/11/18		Do	
"	19/11/18		Do	
"	20/11/18		Do	
"	21/11/18		Do	
"	22/11/18		Do	
"	23/11/18		Do	
"	24/11/18		Do	
"	25/11/18		The Brigade took part in tactical exercise with the 144th Infantry Bde.	
"	26/11/18		Training carried out and work continued on Observation and forward Positions	
"	27/11/18		Do	
"	28/11/18		Brigade tactical scheme carried out. Do	
"	29/11/18		Training carried out and work on Positions continued	
"	30/11/18		Do	
"	31/11/18			

CONFIDENTIAL.

WAR DIARY

of

71st Brigade R.F.A.

Volume 31.

From 1st February 1918.   To 1st March 1918.

WAR DIARY
INTELLIGENCE SUMMARY.
(Erase heading not required.)

Army Form C. 2118.

Place	Date	Hour	Summary of Events and Information	Remarks and references to Appendices
ARRAS	1/2/18		A Brigade Tactical scheme was carried out. 13.Cy. 15th Bde firing (practice). 15th Bde on Observation and Forward Positions was carried on.	
"	2/2/18 3/2/18 4/2/18 5/2/18 6/2/18 7/2/18		Training carried out and work on Observation and Forward Positions continued.	
Avion Corner	8/2/18		7th Brigade relieved the 29th Brigade R.F.A. A section from each battery going in. The rest of the 29th Bde. by the 7th Bde was completed. The guns remaining with the exception of "D" Battery, which had two guns remain. The 7th Bde R.F.A. at the relation of Observation, took over by the 32nd Brigade R.F.A. Gun left in situ. Fraustein and batteries varied out. Visibility good. 12 noon 15 pm N.12 & shelled by	
"	9/2/18		3.0 FRA H.2. Few figures seen. Visibility fair to good. A few moments of movement were during the day in the recently fairly hostile artillery quiet.	
"	10/2/18		Registration and calibration carried out. Hostile trench mortars were active, which registered Monchy was occasionally shelled by 4.2. Rumghit Rd Ray 1.55 to 3 pm N 11 A. was heavily shelled by 4.2 & 5.9 from Gireau Wd. 3.40 – 4.10 pm outskirts of Gireau shelled by 4.2	
"	11/2/18		Hostile Artillery abnormally quiet. Monchy and outskirts received the usual shelling movement formally. Today was observed in neighbourhood of Boiry & Via–en–Artois. Visibility Low. Wind blowing mild.	
"	12/2/18		Hostile battery units. Monchy and support lines O & C. received an occasional 77mm and 4.2. The Cambrai Road Redoubt 8.9 pm shelled by 10.4.2. Visibility very fair. Enemy appeared and volley of the GODFUL was shelled by 77mm from 6.15 to 7.30 am. During the morning the whole of the Dumvall front received an occasional 77mm shell. A 4" HV gun occasionally shelled the Cambrai Rd in Siva.	
"	13/2/18			
"	14/2/18			

WAR DIARY or INTELLIGENCE SUMMARY

Army Form C. 2118.

Place	Date	Hour	Summary of Events and Information	Remarks and references to Appendices
Bury Corner	15/2/18		Hostile Artillery T.M. was active at about 9.50 A.M. but were silenced by our artillery. The Roulers Rd. N/144 - No Entral received 12 H.E.² Shrapnel was answered to reach Roulers Rd. Shelling from H.2 between 1 P.M. and 4.30 P.M. Shell cases received attribution from a 4.2 Battery between 10.15 A.M. to 11.0 A.M. Visibility poor	
"	16/2/18		Hostile Artillery:- Battn. merely received the usual early morning shelling from H.2³ and T.M.m. 1.40 - 3.50 P.M. N11C was shelled by H.2³ direction of Sticam. Rate 1 per min until 3.20, when shelling became at rate of 6 per min until 3.50 when it died down by 3.50 P.M. The major return of the firing was at c/4.1 attended Goretam and thinned Goretam in rear. No damage to Grandl or equipment. Granger B. 9410 reported active at 4.30 + 5.5 P.M. N11C 12 Jan shelled 4.40 in numerous W.9.15 P.M. but Artillery retaliated and registered. 4.40 P.M. 5.16 T.M. 8.9410 was retaliated upon from a suspected Battery Position in O4. 7 P.M. carried on a telephoned shoot upon a suspected Battery Position in O9d. O5c + Burke Street. However a good deal of movement small parties in enemy Great Aerial activity on both sides. Visibility good.	
"	17.2.18		Enemy lines south of Porso - Rochmer Rd Shelling. Some of the battery Registration carried out. Merely received the usual morning shelling. Positions in N11c were shelled with about 350 rounds of 4.2 gun direction of Shiney Amertya was slightly damaged. Shelling commenced 8.25 A.M. and ceased at 11.0 A.M. 2.20 to 2.37 P.M. N11 B+C again shelled with 4.2³ about 100 in all. Great activity displayed by aircraft on both sides. Bombs dropped in direction of Mamines 11.55 P.M.	
"	18.2.18		During the morning movement seen in 09 was dispersed by 18 Pd fire. Hostile Artillery slightly intermittently shelled N12 from front to front with T.M. rn and H.2³ 12.15 to 1.5 P.M. T.M. rn active intermittently by day. Great Aerial activity on both sides	
"	19.2.18		Movement thought the day numerous was engaged. Hostile Artillery of large calibre was winter than usual. Hostile field Artillery displayed greater activity in our forward Support-Line	

WAR DIARY
INTELLIGENCE SUMMARY
Army Form C. 2118.

Place	Date	Hour	Summary of Events and Information	Remarks and references to Appendices
Nieuport	19.2.18		and C.T's, N6 and C were in S.P. and C were in S.P. to Tilloy and 5.9" Aerial activity on both sides was normal.	
	20/2/18		Our own Ammo. dump opposite the 158 A.F.B. Rd & Tilloy Rd RT.O. blown up during the morning on SP No 29th Regt. R.A. Hostile artillery minimally quiet mostly getting the usual intermittent shelling. Visibility very poor owing to mist.	
	21/2/18		Hostile Artillery was very active. Particularly in the Crake area. N6 Central was shelled by 5.9, 4.2 between 8.20 and 6pm. Carrucoma Farm & 4.2 gun in N2.4d direction No 11 Battn. At 12 noon to 4.15 pm shelled N.12.8.91 with 12 in WR. Minny crane in top Ravine intermittent shelling. Between 12 noon and 1.25pm 3no 4.2 Carrucoma Farm fell at N.11.C.9.5.33 from direction of Stankham. From 12 noon till 12.40 regulation was carried out on alum front being forward section of 6/11. 12 to 15. 1.25 destructive fire was carried out on one gun pit. Reinf? gun carriage badly damaged. Shell reaching to pit damaged and surface destroyed. No casualties to personnel. About 10 77mm R/R at 025.25 pm landed OS in N.4 received about 20 59" between 730-755 p.m. During the night there was desultory shelling "track" area. Registration was carried out by our batteries chiefly from front line in O.S.P. Hostile fire of a corps calibre all the battery shelling N.I.C.7.5.33. Visibility in morning poor & German V.A.	
	22/2/18		movement in O.9d was dispersed by our artillery coming in barrage. Registration and infiltration was carried. We had but during the day at O.8d + 8.00. Hostile T.M. were retaliated on and silenced. Twice during the day. Hostile Artillery was below than usual. During the morning a little harassing fire from 77mm was directed on trenches in O.2a. Gunsupport lines in N8 a+c received a few 77mm at midday. Visibility fair to 3.30 p.m.	
	23/2/18		S.O.S fired in expect of Stand in enemy front in O.8c. Green Venels was entered and 3 prisoners secured. We had no casualties. During the morning and afternoon Castle T.M. during our activity. We fired on Bin on Lys 18 pr and silenced minenwerfer. During the day we engaged hostile	

WAR DIARY
INTELLIGENCE SUMMARY
(Erase heading not required.)

Army Form C. 2118.

Instructions regarding War Diaries and Intelligence Summaries are contained in F. S. Regs., Part II. and the Staff Manual respectively. Title pages will be prepared in manuscript.

Place	Date	Hour	Summary of Events and Information	Remarks and references to Appendices
Ring Corner	25.2.18		Hostile artillery was more active than usual. Between 8.15 and 10.00 am N & C TT was subjected to harassing fire from 5.9 and 4.2" and at 60 Rds in all. At 11.20 am Puggs't was again shelled. During the morning N 6 A 8 T was registered by 77mm. Ina Byrne received harassing fire from 77mm in the morning. Mudday Cmtry Trinchy was shelled by 77mm. Bursts in O8 a+c shelled with 5.9". Enfilade destruction fire on T.M. N. Belilih'e Ret. Naval activity below normal.	
	27.4.2.18		Enemy Aadn, 18 Pr fired into the enemy wire at N. 9B. But 4.5 How. registered Point S in O 30 with 60 HC with an aeroplane. Regulation 8 18 Pr was also carried out. an aeroplane. 4.5 Hows in action to N.NF Salt. OD 31 was engaged by our 4.5 Hows immediately with 4.2". This place hostile artillery were having the day registered on a great number of points in N12 and was intermittently shelled also received the usual barranging fire. Landraia Rd in N12, Lunbraia Rd and Ramparts were caused Turnpike Ridge by 77mm from 3.4+5 & 4.25 pm. Guemappe and Vauchelles Road by 4.2 and 5.9".	
	25.2.18		Considerable movement was seen throughout the day which was engaged by our 18 pr. causing several casualties. Somewhat the day hostile T.M. displayed a certain amount of activity along the whole of the divisional front. They were retaliated on by 18 pr and 4.5 Cmps and silenced. Registration was carried out. Intermittently during the day harassing fire by 77mm and 4.2" was directed on N and N12. Oatwalk 1-2 pm a But 4.2 fell Swear Caulvai Rd in N12. A and B. Batteries 158 AFA Brigade joined this sub. group. A Battery Relaying over B/71 alternative position. 15 Rds of the name and detached gunting of 4/70	
	26.2.18		Hostile T.M. were retaliated on and whenever engaged. Hostile Artillery was less keen was usual. Tourley and the Cambrai Rd was slightly shelled in the morning. Between 9:30 am and 2:30 pm T.M. were active in three occasions and were retaliated on by our artillery. Visibility fair.	

WAR DIARY
or
INTELLIGENCE SUMMARY

Army Form C. 2118.

(Erase heading not required.)

Place	Date	Hour	Summary of Events and Information	Remarks and references to Appendices
Vimy Corner	27/2/18		The enemy T.M. were very busy during the morning. Their fire seemed chiefly directed upon our front line in front of TITES COPSE; generally nine shots fired during the morning. A light barrage of T.M. and 4.2" was put down on our support lines between LAMBRA RD. & TITES RD., this being retaliation for our shelling of the enemy T.M. on Munchy and the CAMBRAI line seemed to have been in plain co-operation between also field guns and two 4.2" when a field battery opened fire on our support trenches. T.M° at 11 am beacond T.M° Re-when it commenced. 20 5.9" fell N.of N bA bA b.4, what the firing period of suddenly as it commenced. 20 5.9" fired on H.34 L.4 & mortar apparently registration. Between 2-5 pm 150 Rds 8" & 5.9" fired on H.34 L.4 & mortar aeroplane observation. The usual intermittent shelling of our support lines and communication trenches by T.M. 4 & 2. Our artillery engaged movement through the day causing casualties. Double T.M. were retaliated upon by 18 pr. 4.5 how and 6" a little registration was carried out with 4.5 shells fitted with new drawing fuse. Visibility good after 11 am	
"	28/2/18		Wancourt was shelled with a slow rate by a 4" H.V. gun from 8.15 to 9.15 am. The Cavalerai Rd. and MONCHY came in for the usual intermittent shelling from T.M. and 4.2". Mk 3.20 pm N.ill support and VINE AVENUE was shelled by 5.9" about 20. CRATER SUBWAY received about 50 T.M. between 8.45 & 9.15 pm. T.M. 8, 9 & 10 were increasingly active upon TITES COPSE and our front support lines in O.2.d and O.8.b. but Artillery engaged movement. Ramsfers this morning causing 3 casualties. Aside T.M. here retaliated on and silenced. During the afternoon Registration took place.	

28/2/18

15th Divisional Artillery.

71st BRIGADE R. F. A.

MARCH 1918

CONFIDENTIAL.

WAR DIARY

of

71st Brigade R.F.A.
(Volume 32)

From 1st March 1918. to 31st March 1918.

Army Form C. 2118.

WAR DIARY
INTELLIGENCE SUMMARY.
(Erase heading not required.)

Instructions regarding War Diaries and Intelligence Summaries are contained in F. S. Regs., Part II. and the Staff Manual respectively. Title pages will be prepared in manuscript.

Place	Date	Hour	Summary of Events and Information	Remarks and references to Appendices
Bury/Corres	1-3-18		What little movement seen was engaged. Hostile Artillery was quiet. Munchy and C7M13R91 Rd same as for the usual intermittent shelling. Visibility was poor.	
	2-3-18		A shoup was commenced in the positions of the batteries of this Sub Group. R4B/11 moving from their sheltered returns to the main position at B158. While R4B moved to its alternative position. D/11 commenced to move its main position to B/11 Alternative position. Artillery on both sides was quiet owing to very low visibility on account of snow storms.	
	3-3-18		Throughout the morning movement was engaged by 18 prs and 4.5 hows. Registration and Calibration was carried out. Hostile artillery was quiet. Munchy and the Cambrai Road received the usual intermittent shelled. Movement behind enemy lines where the normal. Probably something is diesamal or regimental relief.	
	4-2-18		Our Artillery. Active T.M. was engaged shewing the morning. Hostile Artillery. Quiet. Visibility low.	
	5-2-18		Dull owing to bad visibility the day was quiet.	
	6-2-18		Our artillery engaged movement throughout the day causing casualties. M-2.45a.m. was fired on and silenced. The raid by the 15 British Rifles, Aust. & TM being very active was fired on and silenced. Palliation and registration carried out. Hostile Artillery was active. 77mm at 2° registered Munchy. Some O.P. mounded third Ext. Hundy Little damage done. Two other O.P.s used by this Brigade and rewisted but support line from MONCHY to C7M15R91 Rd. Heavily heavily shelled with H.E. and 77mm. 106 shown after. Probably retaliation for our fire on TM?	

WAR DIARY or INTELLIGENCE SUMMARY

Army Form C. 2118.

Place	Date	Hour	Summary of Events and Information	Remarks and references to Appendices
Pury Corner	6.3.18		From 10.50 – 11.15 a.m. N.12 & shelled by 4.2" about 18A per min. The Barrage in reply is our road was very heavy from a vicinity of Z.4.4 and firing down at Z.4.5. Aerial Activity was slightly above normal.	
"	7.3.18		Our line: Registration was carried out during the day. Movement engaged and active T.M.s silenced. Hostile Firing during the afternoon mostly light 5.9. 2.30 – 2.55 P.M. G.7.c long 2. 4" H.V. guns. 11 – 11.30 a.m. N.6 & A was harassed by 5.9. 2.30 – 2.55 P.M. G.7.c long Harassed by 12 77mm & 6 4.2" N.12 & Anzac Lane was shelled by 12 4" H.V. between 3.45 – 4.10 P.M. Four occasions during the day hostile T.M. wire cutting in our support lines in O.8 & 9.c. Visibility Good.	
"	8.3.18		Our line: Wire registration and registration carried out. 15 a firing in support front line 2" M. Hostile fire: A little registration was carried out – by 5.9 and 8" on turnery. 10.30 – 11.30 a.m. 30 77mm fire at LA BERGERE. The CAMBRAI Rd in vicinity of CAVALRY FARM was shelled by 60 77mm between 2–4 P.M. Aerial Activity was slightly above normal.	
"	9.3.18		Our line: 18 CH engaged working parties in O.9.d & O.9.c 1 man killed and several casualties caused. Hostile fire: 7.10 – 7.30 a.m. our trenches in O.8.d were shelled by 4.2" & Talk of 2 per min. This shoot was repeated 8 – 8.30 a.m. During the morning MONCHY was registered on three occasions by 4.2" and fire during the afternoon. 2.30 P.M. 20 77mm at N.12.a. Between 12 mid 1.50 P.M. 50 4.2" fire on LA BERGERE. Visibility Good.	
"	10.3.18		Our line: Prominent – The day movement in O.9.c and O.15.a was engaged by 18 pdr and 4.5 How. A Lewis Gun running from O.15.a & O.9.c was under intermittent fire during the night. From 3.15 P.M. to 5.30 P.M. Front at O.14 & 5.9 was steadily shelled.	

WAR DIARY or INTELLIGENCE SUMMARY

Army Form C.2118.

Place	Date	Hour	Summary of Events and Information	Remarks and references to Appendices
Anyhow	10.3.18		Artille Fire :- On a whole Artille Artillery was only fairly active during the morning. A few rds H.E. fell at TITES COPSE, N24d & OBR. 11.15 AM 5 rds 4.2 fell on O16. Visibility poor owing to ground mist.	
	11.3.18		Hostile T.M.s were engaged three times during the day by 18 pr and silenced. Movement was also engaged. 6.15 P.M. we fired in support of the raid carried out by Hostile Artillery was quiet during the morning. 3.15 - 3.55 pm HUSSAR LANE N12 & was shelled by 4.2" 40 in all. 4.40 to 4.50 pm SADDLE SUPPORT and KNIFE TR was shelled by 50 4.2" and T.mm. Hostile T.M. was active upon CAVALRY FARM. PICK AVENUE. TITES COPSE & TROWEL ALLEY. Visibility good.	
	12.3.18		Hostile T.M.s engaged during the day from 9pm to 6 am 13. 18 pr were used not harassing fire on POODLE & FOX TR. Trenches in O3c&d, STIRRUP LANE in O9. BEETLE TR and Trenches in O9 b c&d, FIFE, WHISTLE & 13 RUMLEY TR in O15 n & b. 600 Rds being expended. During same period 4.5 Guns fired upon Trenches in I33d. VERT & GREEN WORK, Dugouts in O9a & d, Dugouts in WHISTLE and FACTORY. 36 LETHAL were fired upon I33 c.q.s MC 8 pm and 11.30 P.M. - Counter Preparation was carried out at following times. 12.15, 3.15, 3.30, 4.30 am 4.50 5.30. 6 am. — 12 mm. Hostile Artillery :- 4.2" and T mm registered on MONCHY and 5.9" on WANCOURT TOWER. 11.40 am 60 4.2 and T mm fell in support lines in O8a being retaliation. 10.50 - 11.30 am 30. 4.2" 25. 5.9° fell on N24d and 11.30 - 12.10 am 20 4.2 on N18. 5-6 pm. 12. 4.2" on N12 & 5-6.15 pm. Fire. During the night enemy made but little retaliation to our harassing fire.	
	13.3.18		Our fire:- Registration took place during afternoon. Hostile T.M.s were silenced. During the night harassing fire was maintained on following points. 600 Rds 18 pdr 600dle was top trench	

WAR DIARY
INTELLIGENCE SUMMARY

Army Form C.2118.

Instructions regarding War Diaries and Intelligence Summaries are contained in F.S. Regs., Part II. and the Staff Manual respectively. Title pages will be prepared in manuscript.

(Erase heading not required.)

Place	Date	Hour	Summary of Events and Information	Remarks and references to Appendices
Pozieres	13.3.18		Trenches in O3c&d STIRRUP LANE in O9, BEETLE TR and Trenches in O9,B,C,d. FIFE WHISTLE BROMLEY in O15a&b. 4.5 Guns fired 108 Rds on Trenches in I33d, VERT & GREEN WOOD dugouts in O9 b & d. Hostile artillery was silent during the morning and displayed some activity during the afternoon. At 2.30 pm and again between 5 to 6 pm a few 77mm fell on the Tambour Rd in N12.G. 3-4 cm intermittent shelling of N12.B. O15 and O9a by 77mm. Villabley Road.	
	14.3.18		18R Line - During the day the following rounds were kept under harassing fire. BADGER - O8d Trenches from O10c,5,4 15 0 and 63. Trenches and Railway from O10d 2,3 to O11d 59. LONG WOOD Trenches in I33d. Distancement in O8a. Railway in O5B. Easter Edge, Bois du VERT. During the night harassing fire was directed upon trenches and trenches by 18 pdrs and trenches and dugouts by 4.5 Hows. Arrival Line - 11.30 28 Rds + 2 BR on CRATER SUBWAY. Between 2 and 4 pm KESTRAL AV, SHOVEL TRENCH and Junction of PICK & SADDLE were harassed by 4.2" about 30 Rds in all. 2.55 pm 20 rds + 2 BR upon O8a b11. At 4.50 and again at 5.15 pm retaliated upon our front line in O8B so Rds in all. Hostile TM were slightly active.	
	15.3.18		Gun fire - During the day 700 18 Pdrs + 108 - 4.5 Hows were fired (harassing) on trenches in I33d & I34c. Eastern outskirts of Bouzy, LONG WOOD & the Railway in O10a + O11c. 130 15 du VERT. Movement was engaged in O15d, O11 & O10 cad and on CAMBRAI RD. During the night the following rounds were kept under fire. Trenches in O9 c & d, O3 & d, Trenches in I33d, Dugouts in O9 b & d. Counter preparation was carried out at 2.15 am, 3.55 pm and 5.45 am. Hostile fire. - Very little activity was displayed by double artillery. 5 rounds and 8 rounds	

WAR DIARY or INTELLIGENCE SUMMARY

Army Form C. 2118.

(Erase heading not required.)

Instructions regarding War Diaries and Intelligence Summaries are contained in F. S. Regs., Part II. and the Staff Manual respectively. Title pages will be prepared in manuscript.

Place	Date	Hour	Summary of Events and Information	Remarks and references to Appendices
Brig Corner	15.3.18		TOWER shelled by 5.9" intermittently throughout the day. Munchy was registered by 5.9" and 77 mm. The area between Saddle and Spade was harassed by 4.2 and 77 mm midday.	
	16.3.18		Snr. Inf:- During the day harassing fire was brought to bear on covered approaches to the enemy front line system. Hostile T.M.s were retaliated upon three times between 12.30 and 1.30 p.m. During the night fire was brought to bear upon trenches and tracks in I.33.d. Trenches in O.3.d & c, O.9.a & c, and VERT WORK. Hostile fire:- 8.45 – 10.10 a.m. 60 4.2" S.R.R. in Ivrea area. This was apparently destructive fire on a 15 pdr Anti-Tank gun placed here. This gun was damaged. 12.20. 30 4.2 and 5.9 SRR near Saddle and Hd Support Line. 12.40 p.m. 60 5.9", 4.2" 77mm S.R.R Support Line. This shoot was again repeated at 1.17 & 1.45 p.m. Probably retaliation for our T.M. bombardment. 2.35 & 3. p.m. 30 4.2" S.R.R. on Rd CAMBRAI R.P. Visibility poor in morning.	
	17.3.18		Snr. Inf :- During the day harassing fire was brought to bear upon tracks and railway in I.33.d, I.34.c & O.10.c.&.d. Installations at BOIRY, LONGWOOD. Bois Fourchu Owl. Bony LANE. During the night harassing fire was maintained upon tracks in I.33.d, I.34.c, O.9.c.&.d. Camouflage at O.9.c and O.4.d. Tracks in O.16.c, O.16.a. Howitzer preparation carried out at zero hour. Hostile fire:- The fire during the day was harassing and only light. Between 2 p.m. & 5.45 p.m. 40 Rds 4.2" S.R.R. on HUSSARD LANE. Sun support Line in O.8 & 4 c. received 4 Runs 4.2" during the day. A large number of Rockets Observation Balloons were up in visibility was good.	
	18.3.18		Snr Inf. Harassing fire was maintained during the day upon the enemy covered approaches. During afternoon 25 Rds Shrapnel was fired at camouflaged dump at O.4.d. b.8. Several	

(A7092) Wt. W28139/M293. 75,000. 1/17. D. D. & L. Ltd. Forms/C.2118/14.

WAR DIARY
or
INTELLIGENCE SUMMARY

Army Form C. 2118.

Place	Date	Hour	Summary of Events and Information	Remarks and references to Appendices
AIRY CORNER	18.3.18		Direct Rifle being obtained, movement was engaged throughout the day, several casualties being caused. 11.30 am Hostile TM were silenced by our fire. During the night we carried out harassing fire and counter preparation.	
	19.3.18		Hostile arty:- Very little activity was displayed by hostile artillery. During the morning 20 Rds 5.9" fell in OB4 & NC2. 1.30 pm WANCOURT TOWERS was registered by 5.9": 4.2" TM. Movement in the could areas was considerable on account of visibility being good & large number of hostile observation Balloons were up during the morning. Our fire. The usual harassing fire was carried out during morning and afternoon. Also counter preparation. Hostile fire:- Between 12 and 12.30 pm N12A was shelled with 20 Rds 4.2", SHIKAR AVENUE with the same number of 5.9". WANCOURT TOWER registered by 77mm & Feuchy Vis-Railway Road.	
	20.3.18		Our fire:- Harassing fire was maintained on all tracks and approaches in the area during day & night linking points on BEETLE, FIFE and approach round HQ on BENT were engaged. Several casualties being caused. Counter preparation was carried out. Hostile fire:- Considerably below normal a 77mm battery registered on Monchy & desultory fire on N14 & 97 with 4.2's	att.

Army Form C. 2118.

WAR DIARY
or
INTELLIGENCE SUMMARY.

(Erase heading not required.)

Instructions regarding War Diaries and Intelligence Summaries are contained in F. S. Regs., Part II. and the Staff Manual respectively. Title pages will be prepared in manuscript.

Place	Date	Hour	Summary of Events and Information	Remarks and references to Appendices
AIRY CORNER.	21.3.16		Our fire:- All batteries of Right Group fired on ASSIST South + carried out Counter preparation Stores	
		9.2 pm to 10.14	We fired on SOS lines as ordered having fired a counter-preparation during both day & night. OB322 was engaged by all batteries & silenced	
		5.5-7.0 am	Hostile fire:- WANCOURT was heavily shelled with gas+HE, also WANCOURT VALLEY. Shelling continued heavily	
			Until 7.0 am when it slackened considerably	
		8.0 am	Another group of hostile batteries commenced searching the ground on either side of THE CAMBRAI ROAD from LABERGERE to FEUCHY CHAPEL corner with HE & gas chiefly 4.2's & 8's This previously ceased at 10am, but commenced again in the afternoon and except for a few short	
			spells continued through the whole day.	
		6.9 am	The enemy launched a projector attack, the firing of which sounded like a lot of guns of small calibre, but all went off together, no casualties were reported	
		6.30 am	The enemy heavily engaged the Gunners on our right.	
		8.7 am	The enemy put down a heavy barrage of 5.9's + 4.2's - 77mm + 77's on our front & support line but no infantry action took place	
			Both sides were kept under fire with H.V. guns causing considerable damage to houses in ARRAS & surrounding villages	R.L.P.
	22.3.16		Our fire:-	
		3.7 am + 1.45 pm to 1.65 pm	Fire on counter preparation	
		9.2 am	at fired on SOS lines	
		9.2 -10.0 am		
			During the remainder of the day we kept up harassing fire on POODLE, FR STIRRUP LANE checker on board-133d-134c BEETLE & FIFE TRS where the enemy were suspected to be massing	
			ORANGES 1-7 were engaged	
		3.30-3.33	We fired on ASSISTSTONE	

Army Form C. 2118.

WAR DIARY
or
INTELLIGENCE SUMMARY.
(Erase heading not required.)

Instructions regarding War Diaries and Intelligence Summaries are contained in F.S. Regs., Part II. and the Staff Manual respectively. Title pages will be prepared in manuscript.

Place	Date	Hour	Summary of Events and Information	Remarks and references to Appendices
AIRY CORNER.	22.3.18		**Hostile Fire:-** Monchy was shelled intermittently all day with 77m from direction of BOIRY. Throughout the whole day WANCOURT & WANCOURT VALLEY were kept under fire having very intense at times. Gas was also used. The enemy carried out harassing fire during the whole day on CAMBRAI ROAD and also some of the batteries, specially the forward section situated in the vicinity of the Lepine Farm.	
			General. During the night no movement to the forward areas #234 3rd system. This was successfully carried out without any casualties.	PA 2.
WILDERNESS CAMP.	23.3.18		At 11.40 the enemy's (movement) agents were seen advancing over ridge E of HUSSAR LANE. and about mid-day he advanced in small parties to CONGO & LES FOSSES FARM.	
			HOSTILE FIRE. Fairly quiet except for HV guns fired on back areas. During the whole day the enemy was harassed with severe enemy movement.	
	12.0		On fire:-	
	2.0 pm		of LES FOSSES FARM. but was driven off by our fire. Later (three) to collect in the valley. What was (reported) by small trench howitzer fire.	S.02.
	24.3.18		**Gun fire:-** All movement was engaged with very good results. suspected battery in VINE & SPADE were engaged and silenced several times during the day. Considerable movement seen on the CAMBRAI ROAD engaged by 16 pdrs. Numerous enemy casualties being inflicted. Harassing fire was carried out during the days & night. Hostile fire chiefly on the CAMBRAI ROAD in the neighbourhood of TILLOY also on back areas.	

71st Bde R.F.A

Page covering period 25th to 27th March 1918 appears to be missing.

Army Form C. 2118.

WAR DIARY
or
INTELLIGENCE SUMMARY.
(Erase heading not required.)

Instructions regarding War Diaries and Intelligence Summaries are contained in F. S. Regs., Part II. and the Staff Manual respectively. Title pages will be prepared in manuscript.

Place	Date	Hour	Summary of Events and Information	Remarks and references to Appendices
WILDERNESS CAMP.	28-3-18	3.30	The enemy put down a very heavy barrage of HE & gas, on the CAMBRAI ROAD & batting positions in H.25.d.&.b. This continued till 6.0am when the enemy was used chiefly 5.9's. A barrage of 4.2's & 5.9's was put down on the front system at 6.0am at at 7.0am the enemy attacked & forced our infantry back to the army line on Observation ridge were the enemy was held up	
		10.05	Our batteries withdrew to positions in Gaza, the remainder keping up their fire till there were no infantry. Batteries withdrew the remainder of the batteries withdrew. During the night harassing was carried out on the CAMBRAI ROAD & PELVES LANE	1842
		1.15	All guns were registered & harassing fire during the night carried out.	242
CEMETERY. ARRAS.	29.3.18		Hostile artillery Excessing 6 Good very little fired being observed.	
			Gas fire. Movement was engaged & harassing fire carried out. Suspected battery positions were hidden. NGC engaged	
	30.3.18		Hostile fire	
		7.0–6.30 am	TILLOY was heavily shelled with 6.9's & 4.2's. ARRAS was heavy shelled with 4.2 & 5.9's, causing casualties during the afternoon. During the hours of 1.0/7/ (?) forward wagon lines coming	
	31-3-18		General. At 11 "D"/71 moved from their position in Gaza to position in S.23a N of the Railway During the day batteries all movement was any engd. batteries in N52 were silenced, ankerpond	
			Gas fire.	

WAR DIARY
or
INTELLIGENCE SUMMARY.

(Erase heading not required.)

Army Form C. 2118.

Place	Date	Hour	Summary of Events and Information	Remarks and references to Appendices
CEMETERY. ARRAS	31/3/18		Brake point at 6 on CAMBRAI ROAD on N3a was fired on by howitzer. During the afternoon a suspected T.M. in H.33 central was engaged. Hostile Shelling: The enemy carried out harassing fire in the forward areas	1892
		11:45am to 10pm	The railway at S.29 a 4.6 was heavily shelled with 8in 5.9 (about 200 rds) considerable damage being done to the surrounding buildings.	

[signature]
Comdr. ? 5.13 R.G.A.

31/3/18

15th Divisional Artillery

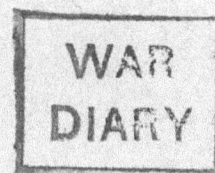

71st BRIGADE R. F. A.

APRIL 1918

CONFIDENTIAL.

WAR DIARY

of

71st Brigade R.F.A.

(Volume 33).

From 1st April 1918.   To 30th April 1918.

Army Form C. 2118.

WAR DIARY
or
INTELLIGENCE SUMMARY.
(Erase heading not required.)

Place	Date	Hour	Summary of Events and Information	Remarks and references to Appendices
CEMETRY. ARRAS.	1/4/18		Gunfire During the day all movement was engaged & guns registered. During the night harassing fire was maintained on roads & tracks. A gas bombardment was carried out on FEUCHY CHAPEL crossroads. In the afternoon the TM in H33 c central was engaged by howitzers on the CAMBRAI ROAD & ARRAS STATION	App.
			Hostile fire Fairly quiet in the morning. During the afternoon the 8"hows were shelling with 4.2's 5.9's 9.3.	
			Aircraft :- Several E.A. flew over ARRAS, one 1 isolated attacks were made on balloon & brought down three of them.	App 2.
		9.35 pm	S.O.S. went up on our right (wire guns were put up). This was followed at 9.45 and later on by gun signals on flares, all were quiet at 10.45 pm. In H32 A & H31	App.
			Artillery or later on by gun signals on flares, all were quiet at 10.45 pm. In H32 A & H31 fire.	
	2/4/18	4 pm 7 pm	Gunfire Movement engaged successfully on H33 a & b along CHAPEL Rd on H33d & H34a. Battery positions on N4d & N5c were shell constantly. During the night harassing fire was maintained on CHAPEL RD H34, H29 cvd, PELVES Lane & Rly battery positions. HALIFAX, CALIFORNIA & ICELAND TR. were swept with bursts of fire.	
		5.30 am	Hostile fire Heavy shelling took place N of SCARPE.	
		7.40 am	Gun lines on H26 & H31 were barraged by 77mm + 4.2's	
		10.30 am/11am	H32 B heavily shelled with 4.2's from MONCHY.	
		6.7.30 pm	CEMETRY & RITZ dumps were slightly shelled with 8" During the night there was spasmodic gas shelling on H 26 & H31	

Army Form C. 2118.

WAR DIARY
or
INTELLIGENCE SUMMARY.
(Erase heading not required.)

Instructions regarding War Diaries and Intelligence Summaries are contained in F. S. Regs., Part II. and the Staff Manual respectively. Title pages will be prepared in manuscript.

Place	Date	Hour	Summary of Events and Information	Remarks and references to Appendices
Artillery ARRAS	3/4/18	Gunfire	During the day all movement was engaged several casualties being inflicted. Harassing fire was maintained during the night on selected targets in H28 and also old billeting positions. HALIFAX & ICELAND TR.	A.A.
		Hostile fire	Fairly quiet. In the morning CAMBRAI ROAD was shelled intermittently with 4.2's & 5.9's. 2/71 moved during the night to a new position in G24a 05.65	R.A.2
		General	Visibility bad. Harassing fire was maintained during the day. During the night harassing fire was maintained	
	4/4/18	Hostile fire	Again fairly quiet. TILLOY WANCOURT ROAD was shelled with 5.9's also the CAMBRAI ROAD.	R.A.3
			During the morning trenches in H25r2d were intermittently shelled with 4.2. A few 8" fell in the ST SAUVEURS area. During the day 13/71 moved to new position at G23c 60	
		General	Bde HQ moved to 20 RUE DES AUGUSTINES. Visibility very poor harassing fire was maintained on enemy's targets on back areas	R.G.
ARRAS	5/4/18	Invisible fire	To counter enemy's troops reported to be relieving at night harassing fire on H.29 & H28. H33 Valley, on H25 & H31 was heavily shelled with 4.2 & 7.7mm. In the afternoon area trenches carried out on G29.	
	6/4/18	Gunfire	6.30am Field Barrage was put down for the Infantry to see exactly nature of wire. Registration of Calibration were also carried out. Battery position at H27A 3.8 were shelled by 4.5 hour	R.A.4
			11am	

WAR DIARY
or
INTELLIGENCE SUMMARY.
(Erase heading not required.)

Army Form C. 2118.

Place	Date	Hour	Summary of Events and Information	Remarks and references to Appendices
	6/4/18		An attempt to est the camouflage at this position was unsuccessful. Movement in H.34 & H.26.c. was successfully engaged.	RGA
	7/4/18		Hostile fire During the morning hostile artillery was very quiet. During the night our raiders carried out along the Railway & in H.25.	RGA
			Gunfire Movement was engaged along FEUCHY CHAPEL road	
			suspected battery positions in N.57 & 10 were silenced	
	8/4/18	12.10 pm	Considerable movement in NOVA SCOTIA trench, relief suspected.	RGA
		8/- pm	During the night hearing fire was vigorously carried out.	
			Visibility was, hampering fire continued through day & following night	
			CAMBRAI ROAD in G.30 & 36 shelled during the afternoon & at 8.40 p.m. Cemetery was shelled	
			with 77mm gas.	
	9/4/18	4.0 am	SOS at a slow rate at a slow rate sweeps forward B.30 & 33.	RGA
		6.30 am	Enemy battery wide was carried and our position in N.8 & N.10 & 11. Enemy fire ordinary	
			Enemy battery work was carried, otherwise shelly blow normal.	
			Hostile fire. Areas H.25. G.30. 36 were shelled during the afternoon, otherwise shelly blow normal.	
			Cemetery was gassed at intervals during the night.	
	10/4/18		No fire on the batteries in N.5 & N.10 with gas reported. Hostile fire considerably below normal. Six shells fell near C's batteries thought to be 15 pdr.	RGA

WAR DIARY
or
INTELLIGENCE SUMMARY.

Army Form C. 2118.

(Erase heading not required.)

Place	Date	Hour	Summary of Events and Information	Remarks and references to Appendices
	11/4/18		Visibility poor. Harassing fire carried on during the day, special attention being paid to TEUILY.	
			CHAPEL ROAD shelled intermittently during the night.	
			Harassing fire carried out during the night.	
	14/4/18		Very little hostile shelling.	
			Ex. OP H 16 a 7.8 was shelled with N.E. front & support lines hostile shelling was below normal.	
			OP H 16 a 7.8 was shelled with 77mm for about an hour.	
			Harassing fires were maintained during the night.	
	13/4/18		Day quiet. Visibility bad.	
	14/4/18		Section rally a.m. of enemy in sap indicated hostile shelling with 77mm & Howitzer & Grenade M.g.	
			Shewn yesterday.	
			Harassing fire carried on during the night.	
	15/4/18		Very quiet.	
			Movement was engaged with good effect.	
	16/4/18		Hostile artillery quiet.	
			Hostile artillery on our front & in a reported H.Q.dq. of Battery.	
	17/4/18		Engaged the Battery in N10 a N5 a. succeeded in silencing them. Moved in large HILL wavey up & 6x95 thing II to be 7 M's fellow observation ridge	
			Hostile fire was suspected.	
	18/4/18		A heavy relief was suspected. Our own shelling in heavy 5 9's hit an artillery helping in general. Gas × was shelling from harras with 5 9's Visibility bad. I shell artillery helping but 3/5 shell fell in the country.	

Army Form C. 2118.

WAR DIARY
or
INTELLIGENCE SUMMARY.
(Erase heading not required.)

Instructions regarding War Diaries and Intelligence Summaries are contained in F. S. Regs., Part II. and the Staff Manual respectively. Title pages will be prepared in manuscript.

Place	Date	Hour	Summary of Events and Information	Remarks and references to Appendices
ARRAS	19/4/18.		[illegible handwritten entry] engaged in D.S.C. & something [illegible]. Thereafter fire returned during the night. 9.22 & 19.2.c stable all day with 59.2 × gas. Observation stopped THROUGHOUT.	897
	20/4/18.		During the day the enemy put a large amount of [illegible] into [illegible] with gas including gas shells & 5.9. The remainder [illegible] range & [illegible]. 305 put up on R1 Bn front where M. [illegible] Counter fire was very successful on 3,191 & 97.2.d.1.9 [illegible] by firing the filling of the 305 D/L two [illegible] retaliation of 9 guns [illegible] & Field gun retaliation detachment 2 had 2 guns - 4 R1 Bn rifles attached [illegible] reinforced by a machine gun - a machine gun detachment in support.	892
	21/4/18.	10.35 11.10 11.10	In the early morning [illegible] to [illegible] report. Brigade Fry. until 3.15 report. Hostile artillery on 9.2.2 + 9.2.3 was attacked [illegible] our own [illegible] the enemy retaliated with hostile artillery on 7 + 8 [illegible] & field artillery + aeroplanes, an [illegible] between 7 + 8 9.30 a.m., the enemy [illegible] [illegible] ups with a [illegible] of 76.9.30.	897 897
	22/4/18			
	23/4/18	1.45 am	Fired in support of Raid by the Canadians, 2 men wounded gun. Harassing fire opened out during the night. Intermittent HE & on from the artillery persisted all day until 4 + 71 on which seemed to be especially close up.	897

Army Form C. 2118.

WAR DIARY
or
INTELLIGENCE SUMMARY.
(Erase heading not required.)

Instructions regarding War Diaries and Intelligence Summaries are contained in F. S. Regs., Part II. and the Staff Manual respectively. Title pages will be prepared in manuscript.

Place	Date	Hour	Summary of Events and Information	Remarks and references to Appendices
	24/4/18		We enjoy a the fatting in N5 - N10 from 9pm to 11pm asking had been execed the enemy a considerable amount of thous with Gas & H.E. During the night several of the men wounded	R42.
	25/4/18		Several enjoyed about every Granaillia through the each morning. Vindictive blown from bug the Bay. Hostile artillery fire, no enemy fire.	R47.
	26/4/18		Infantry moving up at 9pm very close up. Otherwise hostile artillery quiet moderning quiet.	R4.
	27/4/18		Loving gun in Coun really reported a concentration OP on H2G2 shelled with Q's & 77mm guns that afternoon. Fairly loud. Hostile artillery mil.	R47.
	28/4/18			R46.
	29/4/18		Very quiet day. Orders received to move to ANES. arriving	R46.
	30/4/18		BDE moved off at 9-30 to HQ further orders awaited, comfortable billets	R42.

30/4/18
[signature]
Commdt 57 1/10 WR

CONFIDENTIAL.

WAR DIARY

of

71st Brigade R.F.A.

(Volume 34).

From 1st May 1918.

To 31st May 1918.

WAR DIARY or INTELLIGENCE SUMMARY

Army Form C. 2118.

HQ 71 Bde RFA Vol 33

Place	Date	Hour	Summary of Events and Information	Remarks and references to Appendices
ACQ.	1/5/18		Nothing to report	
	2/5/18		Forward section move into the line to relieve the 3rd Can Bde	App 2
	3/5/18		The remaining sections relieved A/71 – 10th 18pr – 11th D/71 – 9th C/71 – 11th ½ Can Batteries	App 2
	4/5/18		Major Grice SI/71 ACB to Brig reporting and assumes his cmd in A26c.	App 2
ROZINCOURT	5/5/18		Registration continued. The following areas received some attention 1316a+d B23.13.1 Central hostile artillery quiet. B72a-c B21a+b.	App 2
	6/5/18		12 LTMS on our flank in TYNE ALLEY. Visibility was very good & considerable harassing fire was engaged by our artillery. Movement was engaged in BOYNE STREET Quarry 7th Avy, & harassing fire was carried on roads, trenches to 135, 6, 7, 412, C 7.8.14. Hostile fire was active above normal T26c was steadily shelled with 15cm from 9am to 2pm 300 rounds 95 was fired onto Railway 42.5 - 59.5 200 rounds 77 mostly smoke were fired on Railway embankment in T26c	App 2
	7/5/18		Visibility being bad, harassing fire was carried out throughout the day on track areas & rendezvous, OPs. Hostile artillery only moderately active. SUGAR FACTORY - OOSE ALLEY - TIRED ALLEY received attention.	RPT
	8/5/18		A working party in B6c was engaged with rounds & redeem on account of mist. Registration carried out during the afternoon & harassing fire about 50 4.2s big fired. JARIBUS WOOD received attention about 50 4.2s big fired. T.M. were active upon B21a between 2.30-3.0 pm.	RPT

WAR DIARY or INTELLIGENCE SUMMARY

Army Form C. 2118.

Place	Date	Hour	Summary of Events and Information	Remarks and references to Appendices
Bois Nieppe	9/5/18		Between 6 p.m. & 10.30 p.m. 400 rds were fired on the OPPY-GAVRELLE ROAD, C.13 central as a relief was thought to be in progress. Harassing fire was carried during the night on ROAD & TRENEWS in the area C.13.d.4 Gas was also fired at selected targets. Hostile artillery was a trifle more active than hitherto, most of which was thought to be registration.	R.S.2.
"	10/5/18		Visibility very good all day. Hostile artillery quiet except for about 10 rounds 4.2 & 5.95 on B.18.a+b. Harassing fire was carried out during the night on selected targets.	R.S.2.
Robecourt	11/5/18		A quiet day. Hostile artillery very normal below normal.	
	13/5/18		Visibility very good, considerable movement seen & engaged. Hostile artillery fairly quiet on selected targets. Harassing fire carried out during the night on selected targets. Very few men or movement, los fires or movement during the day. Harassing fire was seen.	R.S.2.
	14/5/18		Hostile artillery below normal. Loss fired on area shot from C.13.a.0.0 to C.13.a.0.6 Sucrerie track and on selected targets, including at area shot from 400 yds. Slight increase in H. A. whilst shelling of a battalion about concentrated our battery position A.29.a.10 about 50 rds HE expended. very little damage was done. Considerable movement was seen behind NEUVIREUIL which was engaged. There were a number of E.A. over our lines	R.S.2. R.S.2.
	15/5/18			

WAR DIARY
or
INTELLIGENCE SUMMARY.

Army Form C. 2118.

Place	Date	Hour	Summary of Events and Information	Remarks and references to Appendices
Roclincourt	17/5/18		A/71 established a lone gun at B.15.c.15 & B.C. batteries with Director over of their forward guns B/71 moving their waggon gun to B.19.a.9.8. Hostile fire slightly abnormal. WILLERVAL was heavily shelled with 5.9's at 4.40 p.m. Nour[?] was engaged during the day & harassing fire carried out during the night. One Salvo 77(HE?) on Osolette[?] heights.	288.
	18/5/18		Hostile fire rather more active during the late a.m. a 4.2 HV. batty in the vicinity of GLOSTER WOOD being particularly active. approx. about 300 rds into A.23.d. but otherwise very little damage. Light minnewerfer had all day, harassing fire was carried out as usual. No heavies fire was heard during the night.	289.
	19/5/18		A well dug in battery position at C.26.d.7.1.2 neutralised.	
	20/5/18		A/71 fired on battery position at C.26.d.7.1.2 neutralised. A little movement seen in CHALK QUARRY 0202. COULANE & successfully engaged. Harassing fire was carried out.	292.
	21/5/18		A/71 send a gun to the range at GOUY SERVINS for calibration. One of our planes came down in B.32.d. & flame set on fire by own artillery "A 2 BVA received considerable attention from hostile guns 5.9 3+8"	288.

WAR DIARY or INTELLIGENCE SUMMARY

Army Form C. 2118.

Place	Date	Hour	Summary of Events and Information	Remarks and references to Appendices
Richmond	22/5/16		During the day H.Q.s at Bria 9.5.15 + B11 64.1, new work in vicinity of B11 b 7.6.5 + Road from B35c 6.0 – 4.5 to B5 c.9.2.9.D. Enemy Rif't under observn. fell all day of Juney the Light, at the request of the Infantry. Moderately accurate fire of field batteries against the night returned by the enemy but was carried out mostly at night. Hostile fire very much lighter.	
	23/5/16		Moderate harassing of TETTIN', CONNIE TRENCHES also NEW SWITCH + ROUND LINE. Our fire for 5 minutes S.O.S. hostile response to retaliation. Though late no S.O.S. signals. Have very few rounds and carry the night. Hostile battery very quiet.	R.Gd.
	24/5/16		Air fire on BOYNE STREET – Z TRENCH SEVERN VALLEY + CRUCIFIX CORNER also retaliation front trenches from the telephone post Harassing fire during the night. RGC H.Q. was shelled with a few 4.2 H.V. Hostile fire considerable among the hostile batteries. 2 rounds fell in T75 LU3 + A18 d + 11 d 33 B.99.	
	25/5/16		We retaliated on the enemy trenches for trench mortar & gun fire and super front support & rear in B.10.a + B.11c + B.11 d. nr. shells. Harassing fire at night. Hostile artillery very active at 4:00am our front retired from 10 rd + B11 d nr. shells with 77.4.2. 5.95 = 8 and bombardment ceased at 11.45am. Throughout the day up to 11.30pm F18 was severely punished by a 4.2 H.V. gun. It 2 hr. signalling the 5.95 altogether about 60 rounds fell mostly 5.95 with a few 77 rds o 1 gun mostly little damage.	eg2

Army Form C. 2118.

Army Form C. 2118.

WAR DIARY
or
INTELLIGENCE SUMMARY.
(Erase heading not required.)

Instructions regarding War Diaries and Intelligence Summaries are contained in F. S. Regs. Part II. and the Staff Manual respectively. Title pages will be prepared in manuscript.

Place	Date	Hour	Summary of Events and Information	Remarks and references to Appendices
Richmond	27/5/18		Movement has engaged in the usual places. Our aeroplane shoot was carried out with D/M on OPPY CROSS ROAD & the CEMETERY. Harassing fire was carried out during the night. Hostile fire considerable below normal.	RDD.
	28/5/18		E A day active during the night view back areas. Battery at H.26.d.6.2 was engaged on several occasions on ordered. Movement at O.C.d.4.e. was engaged on several Batteries. Hostile artillery quiet, chiefly on A.9.c. with 8" & 5.9. Desultory fire carried out during the night.	RDD.
	29/5/18		A successful aeroplane shoot was carried out by D/M on the cemetery at B yd. Ammunition dumps were carried out by trench mortars and were thought to be dumps, no explosions observed. Movement & parties was engaged on the NEUVIREUIL - 1252 road at two points in C.29.c. The junction of OUSE ALLEY & the German front line was kept under steady fire during the day, a T.M. was suspected at this spot. Harassing fire was carried out on selected targets during the night. Hostile artillery fairly quiet. A number of flashes & shells were taken of hostile batteries in action.	R92.

Army Form C. 2118.

WAR DIARY
or
INTELLIGENCE SUMMARY.
(Erase heading not required.)

Instructions regarding War Diaries and Intelligence Summaries are contained in F. S. Regs., Part II. and the Staff Manual respectively. Title pages will be prepared in manuscript.

Place	Date	Hour	Summary of Events and Information	Remarks and references to Appendices
Richebourg	30/5/18		Visibility very good. Dronewood was engaged during the evening in B6d - B12d - COKE TRENCH T.M. at B11d 80.85 was engaged during the day with ebbeach C7. Harassing fire was carried out during the night. Hostile infantry and M.G. fire was active on CAUSEWAY and TURKEY. Hostile artillery fairly active, especially on FARBUS WOOD. E.A. very active.	B.92.
	31/5/18		A171 mining began to B19 & 45.15 in account of hostile shelling on TRAMWAY HOUSE ALLEY which was very heavy during the day. 570 rounds 4·2 fired in the vicinity. Dronewood was engaged in the usual places. Harassing fire carried out at night.	B.92.

[signature]
31/5/18 Comdg 2 CR

C O N F I D E N T I A L.

W A R   D I A R Y

OF

71st Brigade R.F.A.

(volume 35)

From 1st June 1918.   To 30th June 1918.

WAR DIARY or INTELLIGENCE SUMMARY

Army Form C. 2118.

VSE 34

Place	Date	Hour	Summary of Events and Information	Remarks and references to Appendices
ROCLINCOURT	1/6/18		Harassing fire was carried out between 11pm & 2am. 3am - 4am. Hostile artillery fairly active. Destructive shoot on battery in B24d with 5.9's no damage.	297
	2/6/18		Movement was engaged in the usual places. During the night harassing fire was carried out between 1.30am & 3.0am. At 11pm a lethal shell bombardment of Headquarters & dumps at C.20.a.95.40. B.52.c. carried out with gas shells 2.15am to 4 am. Hostile artillery very active, the whole area heavily shelled with gas & H.E. throughout. Blue Cross & Yellow Cross all calibres being used, also a large amount of phosgene.	297
	3/6/18 & 4/6/18		Movement engaged at B.30.d & 60.b. Y.27.d.B.27.a.09.99. except the night. Enemy had great activity on tracks & centres of activity. Harassing fire was carried out. At 3.10am a refugees on Grenade D for 5 minutes. Artillery activity above normal. B.3.c was shelled with gas.	297 297
	4/6/18		At 7.45pm Grenade 'D' was carried out by forward guns on sector of parties on ridges. Harassing fire was carried out during the night on the ARLEUX-BOIS BERNARD ROAD. Movement was engaged in perpetration for the gas team on C12 C20a. Hostile artillery above normal.	297
	6/6/18		Harassing fire on the ARLEUX-BOIS BERNARD ROAD. Hostile artillery, between 9am & 10am battery areas in A.18 & 24 were subjected to an intense bombardment by 5.9's & 6" – about 300 rounds being put down.	297

WAR DIARY
or
INTELLIGENCE SUMMARY.

(Erase heading not required.)

Army Form C. 2118.

Place	Date	Hour	Summary of Events and Information	Remarks and references to Appendices
	7/6/18		Movement was engaged on Gd ahead C14.O.8.2 a C1C. A machine gun emplacement or O.P. at B12.a.05.80 was shelly & knecked out. Harassing fire during the night on the MAREUX.8015 BERNARD road. Hostile artillery was normal during the period, but singularly inactive during the night except for a few rounds gas in and near a TONY.	R.9.J.
	8/6/18		During the night we fired in engagement with the discharge of gas 2,850 cylinders along the night we fired & little gas bury the night off on B326.c. Hostile artillery fairly quiet.	R92.
	9/6/18		Moved in. C2 control, R808 & R809 Front Red North Hostile artillery very inactive, considerable movement of trains seen on track across.	R92.
	10/6/18		Movement engaged on the usual places. Harassing fire 5 times but less than 300 on trackes & centres of activity.	R9J.
	11/6/18		Movement engaged during the enemy. Harassing fire carried out during the night on trackes – Cuches of activity – Dumps. 18 guns engaged firing H.E. H.O.1 & 7.a.29.21 were bombarded with gas at 1.15. Hostile artillery (below normal).	R.9.J.
	12/6/18		Considerable movement seen on track across. Hostile artillery very quiet.	R.9.J.
	13/6/18		Quiet day. Harassing fire at night.	R.9.J.
	14/6/18		Movement engaged at C15.c.20.40, Cook, C13d bombs in all lines across. At 12-5 a.m. 4 phos gas chemical shell in conjunction with the Chinese Gas Screen.	R9.J.

WAR DIARY
or
INTELLIGENCE SUMMARY.
(Erase heading not required.)

Army Form C. 2118.

Place	Date	Hour	Summary of Events and Information	Remarks and references to Appendices
Richmond	15/6/18		Hostile Artillery very quiet. Harassing fire carried out over the night.	R97.
"	16/6/18		Hostile Artillery quiet. One section moved out with guns to engage line retiring by	R97.
"	17/6/18		Hostile Artillery quiet. Remainder of the batteries moved to wagon line. 258 Bde	R97.
			Bde HQ to ECURIE.	R97.
ECURIE.	18/6/18		Training & Competitions	R97.
	19/6/18		"	R97.
	20/6/18		"	R97.
			One section per battery relieved the batteries of 36 Bde & 2nd D.	R97.
ST NICHOLAS	21/6/18		Relief completed. Guns taken over in situ & harass at Rd.	R97.
	22/6/18		Registration carried. 4.2 battery in Izel silenced by 4-5 hours 15pdr. Harassing fire at night.	R97.
	23/6/18		Slight increase in hostile shelling but still considerably below normal. Registration & some retaliation carried out. No harassing fire. Hostile artillery very quiet.	R97.
	24/6/18		11.30 pm — an outpost of the KOSB 8 prisoners. On duty flying	R98.

Army Form C. 2118.

WAR DIARY
or
INTELLIGENCE SUMMARY.
(Erase heading not required.)

Instructions regarding War Diaries and Intelligence Summaries are contained in F. S. Regs., Part II. and the Staff Manual respectively. Title pages will be prepared in manuscript.

Place	Date	Hour	Summary of Events and Information	Remarks and references to Appendices
St Quilidas	25/6/18	9.30 am	KITTEN 2 reported actions & prisoners. Harassing fire by night. Hostile artillery quiet during the day but heavy gas shelly during the night of H7 central, ATHIES OAM TRENCH in HIGH PARK HILL. YELLOW CROSS. Very little movement seen in this sector in range.	Apt.
	26/6/18		Harassing fire on roads & tracks during the night. Hostile artillery quiet, gas shelling of H7d with YELLOW CROSS during the early hours of the morning but made to our own lines except of a very hostile aircraft active. Much flying to the evening, well directed fire of the AA batteries kept altitude owing to the excessively well directed fire of the AA batteries in this sector.	Apt.
	27/6/18		Divisional arms engaged at the CHEMICAL WORKS & D71 (?) with gun effect on CORONA. Gun fig. bd. Harassing fire carried out during the night between 8 am & 10.0 p.m. all forward guns cooperated in a bombardment of CORONA in support during for 10 minutes put an intense rate. Hostile artillery quiet except in the evening when BLANCK PARK received 150-35 Gas shelly during the night of H7d YELLOW CROSS.	Apt.

(A7092). Wt. W12859/M1293. 750,000. 1/17. D. D. & L., Ltd. Forms/C.2118-14.

CONFIDENTIAL.

WAR DIARY

of

71st Brigade R.F.A.

(Volume 36.)

From 1st ~~July~~ Aug. 1913.   To 31st ~~July~~ Aug. 1913.

WAR DIARY
or
INTELLIGENCE SUMMARY.

Army Form C. 2118.

Place	Date	Hour	Summary of Events and Information	Remarks and references to Appendices
St Quentin	28/6/18		At 5.0 am KITTEN 5 was engaged. During the night harassing fire was carried out on tracks, ways & dugouts. At 12.15 am WELFORD TRENCH was harassed with gas shells. Hostile artillery was very quiet during the day. MUSKETRY VALLEY area shelled with 9.2 How. ORRS fired 10 rgs a gp of DH1. about 100 rounds.	RR7
	29/6/18	6.10 am 4.30	A/71 registered. Three hostile batteries south harbour & sunken will gone silence. 4 pm NF and J.13.d.1-7 were engaged with 15 pdr 4.5 Hows. 5.30 Enemy was heard of LFB cross but. During the night heavy harassing fire was carried out. Battery at H.25.a.20 be neutralised several times during the day 15 pdrs. KITTEN 5 was engaged at abnormal [shoots]	RR+ RR+
	30/6/18	1.0 p-	Harassy fire carried out during the night. Hostile fire normal.	

...Major

Army Form C. 2118.

71st Bde
Vol 35

WAR DIARY
or
INTELLIGENCE SUMMARY.
(Erase heading not required.)

Place	Date	Hour	Summary of Events and Information	Remarks and references to Appendices
St Nicholas	1/7/18		Our fire. We engaged movement near JIGSAW WOOD at range of 7000x also all the Chemical Works were continuous intermittent movement could be seen. During the night harassing fire was carried out on tracks & centres of activity in the area.	1827.
	2/7/18		Hostile fire. Very quiet, below to normal. Three hostile batteries were registered by APM with fellow observation. Their success. Smoke still had to be used for the first two or three observations. Camouflage at I.13.a.9.5, I.5 + I.3.d.8.2. was engaged & several hits obtained. During the night harassing fire was carried out by selected targets. Hostile fire was chiefly Schrecks against the trenches in H11 + H9+10 but was at no time heavy.	1827.
	3/7/18		TM's H9 9+10 were rather active & we co-operated with the Brigade in night strafes them completely. (registered during the morning) Hostile batteries No IC.16 + IC.4.20 were answered IA NF 65 mostly OK's reports. HD NF 52. HID NF. H.36 a + Q.35. HID NF. H36a 40.35. Three NF cells were answered during the night.	
	4/7/18		Harassing fire some carried and quiet throughout the day. Hostile artillery very quiet throughout the day. Two OPs at I.14.d 90.38 + I.14. b 75.14. several direct hits were obtained. TM in H12.c. was engaged.	

WAR DIARY
or
INTELLIGENCE SUMMARY
(Erase heading not required.)

Army Form C. 2118.

Place	Date	Hour	Summary of Events and Information	Remarks and references to Appendices.
St Nicholas	4/7/18		Considerable movement was seen on track areas during our front to the extremity giving visibility. Enemy Artillery fire during the night.	Apps.
	5/7/18		Hostile artillery was very quiet. TM's HB 59.7 were silenced. The follow'g NF add. were ammunn. IA NF 1g a 3.6 & HD ANF H29.50.80. At 8.36pm. The SOS lines were tested found to be correct. During the night hearing fire was very frequent, activity between 10.0pm - 2.0am on the approaches between the SCARPE & the ARRAS-DOUAI Railway. Hostile artillery was quiet during the day but showed marked activity during the night, on back areas between 2.30am & 5.0am 3shrapnel his supposed? Rand were shell? with TM's m 4+2	Apps.
	6/7/18		Gun fire. The camouflage at I.33 d.4.5 was engaged successfully, engaged at I.7d. Movement successfully engaged between followed. at 6.30pm TM at HB.567 were silenced. Hostile batteries at JC11 was registered with balloon observation. Hostile batting at JC11 was the harassing fire was no cooperation with the Gas Beam. 3 days fire ans from 5/7/8 the first favourable opportunity which was to other places in the first favourable opportunity. Hostile artillery rather more active during the afternoon on H71 c & HB set? During the afternoon TM were very active during the afternoon on H71c & HB set? Slight hostile engaged 1/4 HB 3.4.5 3.45pm HB 526 5.14pm HB 1.2. 6.50pm 6+7 No harassing fire during the night.	Apps.

WAR DIARY
or
INTELLIGENCE SUMMARY.

(Erase heading not required.)

Army Form C. 2118.

Place	Date	Hour	Summary of Events and Information	Remarks and references to Appendices
St Nicholas	8/7/18		During the day the following targets were engaged. M.G. located in front of H.2.d 9.3.27 the infantry was led round by O.P. at I.17.d.4.4. Cross roads in I.7.c registered — white flags at I.7.b.4.8 suspect M.G. Bridge at I.20.d 6.0.8.5 tried but obtained T.M.'s H.13.5 – H.12 between 10pm + 1am on roads + tracks.	
	9/7/18		Heavy fire between 10pm + 1am on roads + tracks. An A.V. Battery was engaged at I.19.a 6.0.2.5. effectively silenced.	
		9.0am	H.13.b.4 was dealt with at 6.15. H.12 was silenced. Harassing fire during the night on tracks.	
		9.30pm	night firing in conjunction with raid on Bois Caye position. Quiet after. Barrage fire was continued till 6½ minutes after ZERO hours. finished.	
	10/7/18		I.C.20 was very active all day mostly of low impacts by fits heavy artillery at times, suffered considerable casualties. Enemy trench mortars were often in must have suffered. A.A. battery in PELVES fired a shell whenever active. Harassing fire after the 9pm. Hostile artillery except for I.C.20 was fairly quiet.	
	11/7/18		Our own was engaged in I.7.a + H.12 and also at the CHEMICAL WORKS. Several hits were obtained on O.P at I.14.a 4.0.5.5. MARCHS DOUAI railway. Harassing fire on tracks + roads south of the SCARPE. Hostile artillery very quiet mostly quiet.	
	12/7/18		No harassing fire during the night. Hostile artillery exceedingly quiet.	

WAR DIARY
or
INTELLIGENCE SUMMARY.

(Erase heading not required.)

Army Form C. 2118.

Place	Date	Hour	Summary of Events and Information	Remarks and references to Appendices
Gd Rullecourt	10/7/18		Divisional engaged in line 026 & Gaspards O.P. at I.15.d.0.1 has proved during the afternoon.	
			Mervous MG activity carried out between 10 pm & 2 am.	
			A little hme transport seen in back areas.	
			Considerable enemy and hostile artillery especially in H7d & H8c.	
	15/7/18		Relieved by the 2nd Canadian Bde & marches to ACR Phat night.	
	16/7/18		Entrained at 12.0 m.d. night A.B.C. & 8HV D at AUBIGNY to join 22 Corps.	
	17/7/18		Detrains at 8.0 pm HQ at PONT ST MAXENCE & march to ST MARTIN LONGUEAU.	
	18/7/18		A.B.C.D. detrains during the day & marches to ST MARTIN LONGUEAU. We are now in the 3rd French Army reserve.	
	19/7/18		At 8.0 am marches to VERBERIE. Camped in the FORET DE COMPIEGNE near CROIX ST OUEN.	
	20/7/18		Marches at 7.30 am to VIEUX MOULIN	
	21/7/18		Marches at 6.0 am to RETHEUIL.	
	22/7/18		Marches at 11.3 am to SOUCY - COEUVRES area. 1 section per battery when up to reinforce the 4 & 118 field artillery Regiment forming the 20th French Corps 10th Army.	
Hazelle	23/7/18		Remaining sections of the Batteries marched into Achin in the vicinity of CHAZELLE during the night - wagon lines at DOMMIERS.	

WAR DIARY or INTELLIGENCE SUMMARY

Army Form C. 2118.

Place	Date	Hour	Summary of Events and Information	Remarks and references to Appendices
CHAZELLE	24/7/18		Battns. busy Registering. Hostile Artillery very active at 9-11 P.M. S.O.S. signals sent up. Fire ceased at 9-37 P.M.	Ack L.G.
"	25/7/18		At 4 A.M. all Batteries engaged Buzancy (BUZANCY) & fired S.I. began him. – Hostile Arty very active. On Path W."C". Adj. exploding a small dump. At noon an 8" shell hit C "Adj position wounding L/Bomdr & men. – at 8.45 P.M. another shell hit "C" Adj. wounding Sgt Morrison. – All Batteries carried out Harass'g fire during the night. At 4-30 A.M. S.O.S. signals went up & Batteries answered "D"Adj. anti-aircraft had one shot destroying by high Reference during the day to formation.	Ack L.G.
"	26-7-18		Hostile Batteries were engaged by high Reference during the day. "D"Battery moved its position. – Hostile Shelling was most active all day intermittent in Telagille Valley they were except B 4.25 & 5.0's Shell boxes – "A" Adj. O.P. was heavily Shelled the enemy kept up a hot harassing fire at all hours. There was great aerial activity – the Front Areas as not free from enemy to sub down from flying low. At 4.55 P.M. One Battery fired on to Oruglis, with M.G. in placement on NOYANT. – The enemy fired a great quantity of Gas Shell. This started about 12 of MIDNIGHT (Chiefly in MISSY-aux-BOIS) quantity fell about the Chazelle Valley. (CHAZELLE)	Ack L.G.

WAR DIARY
or
INTELLIGENCE SUMMARY.
(Erase heading not required)

Army Form C. 2118.

Place	Date	Hour	Summary of Events and Information	Remarks and references to Appendices
CHAZELLE Valley	27/7/18.		The Hun has been fairly active against the last 24 hours employing 4.2 - 5.9's and one 8" shell in the Chazelle Valley. To these which a Trent Mont: he country Battery took action being engaged. Aerial activity not so great. Visibility poor. Heavy Rain. S.W.	
do.	28/7/18.		Less activity during day's though on the part of the Hun - Weather Breaks - hues Cork Battery asked the help of our Batteries. 12-20 on enemy obstructing the advance on Burgundy City. Harassing fire started for about 25 minutes. Later 5 Batteries P.M.G. SOS was replied to about 10 minutes. Later, a Coy officers of the Buffs' R02 SOS was regestered. Individual prisoner say our Artillery is most deadly 200 prisoners stating Battalions were compelled to pay almost double their original ratione & Victuals were compelled to share fact of their original Provision through the partial of the Coy. on our right	
do	29/7/18.		The Hun has been very active today harassing our front the back & shelly our Valley. Nearly also our front & the back of shelly our Valley. nearly also our front & the back areas - mostly in gunite. Rained to the brave a storm of Steel gun fire. The enemys aircraft are very active. But the French A.A. are not active here. The Boche has on forward 6 new Active Guns. Kneevry gives him hardly F. 0. when going South a sort of gas - Lad of	

WAR DIARY
or
INTELLIGENCE SUMMARY.
(Erase heading not required.)

Army Form C. 2118.

Instructions regarding War Diaries and Intelligence Summaries are contained in F. S. Regs., Part II. and the Staff Manual respectively. Title pages will be prepared in manuscript.

Place	Date	Hour	Summary of Events and Information	Remarks and references to Appendices
CHAZELLE VALLEY	30/7/18		Brigade Headquarters having been ordered not to remain in the area of a piece of the Valley which had been more Gas shelled than any other, moved in the early hours into to "Relieved B" & "D" Nests with H.Q. Gasalarm - The enemy's aeroplanes were very active during the day flying quite low over Chazelle Valley neighboring hills - The A.A. guns did not engage them - The Valley was bombarded for Gas bombs at night.	E.W.E.G.
do	31/7/18		The enemy has been more active being shelly across back area with 77mm 4.2 & 5.95 - The CHAZELLE VALLEY received several shots during the day - The enemy were no longer to to shelled back in the occasion were met with A.A. fire. The enemy to fire Gas shells on our Batteries during the evening & night - he carried out on Hostile Batty during the night	E.W.E.G.

R.S.Elliott Major RFA.
comdg 71st Bde R.F.A.

C O N F I D E N T I A L.

WAR DIARY.

of

71st Brigade R.F.A.

From 1st August 1918.   To 31st August 1918.

(Volume 37).

Army Form C. 2118.

WAR DIARY
or
INTELLIGENCE SUMMARY.
(Erase heading not required.)

No. 36

Place	Date	Hour	Summary of Events and Information	Remarks and references to Appendices
CHAPELLE VALLEY	1/8/18		During the last 24 hours the enemy has continued to shell Chapelle Valley. He shelled our HQ area with a heavy shelling. At 5:30 p.m. the enemy artillery was quiet. At 9 p.m. our infantry attacked several enemy posts in the support of the attack. Enemy aircraft was very active and our A.A. engaged them every & again this morning. Driven off around O.P. later. Whilst the enemy were operating I was engaged by one of our 18 pdr Batteries who fired several periods of enfilading shells and claimed to have brought down a [?]. Our Drills carried out Manoeuvre and Gaslis Dr Play work.	A.R.L.G.
"	2/8/18		After a night of constant shelling Zero Sharp of the enemy - No guns appeared to come firing about dawn. At 8:30 orders was received that the Germans had evacuated Bayonet & Rogers that our Infantry was moving forward. Our Battery fire was light and was not engaged. Enfilade more distant targets. Our Infantry had succeeded in advancing two officers to advance with the Infantry for the purpose of making a reconnaissance & keep in touch with us. Orders were at once issued for

WAR DIARY
or
INTELLIGENCE SUMMARY.

Army Form C. 2118.

(Erase heading not required.)

Place	Date	Hour	Summary of Events and Information	Remarks and references to Appendices
			As the Williams, the trench relief having been completed but the dawn not broken, Coy. Bn. Batteries had each fired a minimum of 150 rounds of shrapnel while enemy were in the Deniere or nearby CHAZELLE VALLEY were ordered to the bayou huts at DOMMIERS. — The rest of the day & night was utilized in moving ammunition	
3/8/18 DOMMIERS			at CHAZELLE VALLEY to DOMMIERS & to the D.A.C. dump — Orders were received to march at a moments notice for PONT S. MAXENCE.	A.W.L.G.
			to RULLY, enroute for PONT S. MAXENCE.	A.W.L.G.
4/8/18 BARBERIE			The Brigade marched to RULLY, & were informed by fields wire at BARBERIE 2 Kilos distant.	A.W.L.G.
5/8/18 SARRON			The Brigade marched to SARRON via PT ST MAXENCE & ordered to entrain at PT. ST MAXENCE about 7 am. 6/8/18.	A.W.L.G.

WAR DIARY or INTELLIGENCE SUMMARY

Army Form C. 2118.

Place	Date	Hour	Summary of Events and Information	Remarks and references to Appendices
	6/8/18		at 1 A.M. The Headquarters started entraining at PONT	
En Route			ST MAXENCE. The Brigade Group detrained period.	
FREVENT.			8½ - reaching FREVENT at 6-30 P.M.	W.L.9.
	7/8/18		"A" "B" & "C" Batteries each received one Army Horse June	
			Billeted here. "D" Battery marched to its billets	W.L.9.
BERLENCOURT.			at SARS-LE-BOIS.	
	8/8/18		Rest. Clean harness, clothing parades & baths.	
	to			
	15"			
	16"		Inspection for battery reliefs 281 Bde in the line near ARRAS.	
	17"		Reconnaissance relief complete.	R.9.
	18"		Registration carried out by all batteries.	
			Harassing fire at night on roads & tracks.	
			Enemy Artillery very quiet.	
ARRAS.	19"		Few enemy barrages in preparation north of the attack on TOMIAN & ICELAND	R.9.3
			trenches.	
			Machine guns were trouble & engaged.	
			No measures hostile artillery.	
			30 meagre in hostile (Henry shells) with yellow Cross gas about 2000 engrs 35	R.9.2

WAR DIARY or INTELLIGENCE SUMMARY

Army Form C. 2118.

Place	Date	Hour	Summary of Events and Information	Remarks and references to Appendices
ARRAS.	21st		Divs in co-operation with operations on I Corps front fired forward lines in the following targets DOUGLAS trench, ORKNEY trench, BILL trench & SUNKEN Road N3C 7.0.10.4.3. N14.d.25.4.0. The following NF call were answered during the day, N.F. N352 – N353 – N340 – N367. Harassing fire during the night, also gas shell CALIFORNIA & HALIFAX trenches. ARRAS was heavily shelled during night.	Mt.
	22nd		Harassing fire carried out during the night.	app.
	23rd		Hostile artillery exceedingly inactive. Armistice in operation by the VI Corps & firing on Sunken Rd N25.6.6.7 – N32.a.4.6. ARRAS shelling during the night.	app.
	25th		Between 3.55pm & 4.25pm ARRAS VI Corps by firing on DOUGLAS TRENCH & "AIRY WORKS".	
	26th		Moved to battle position on the NEUVILLE VITASSE ROAD	Cp.
	26th	3.0am	Div's creeping barrage in support of the attack on ORANGE HILL & MONCHY.	
		11.0am	Moved forward & took up positions on the South of CAMBRAI road just east of FEUCHY CHAPEL corner.	Cp.
	27th	9.30am	Div's barrage in support of attack on VISENARTOIS moved forward about 12 Corps night Hd quarters in O.13.b. SOUTH of CAMBRAI Road W of CAVALRY FARM.	

WAR DIARY
or
INTELLIGENCE SUMMARY.
(Erase heading not required.)

Army Form C. 2118.

Place	Date	Hour	Summary of Events and Information	Remarks and references to Appendices
	28	12:30	Fired barrage in support of attack on the DROCOURT-QUEANT line. Attack held up by wire in front of OLIVE trench. Continued firing all day, amount of ammunition expended 19,500 rds. 18pr. fires inside the by-laws of the Corps operations.	192
	29		The attack guns registration registered.	
	30	4.40am	Fires protective barrage on OLIVE TRENCH in support of attack on 31st UPTON WOOD, attack successful to 4500 forward.	192 / 193
	31		Moved from position 0.14 forward to 0.28 a+d + 0.22.d.	

E.S. Willett Major R.F.A.
Comdg 4/102 Brigade. R.F.A.

Hqrs 15th Dn. Confidential

Herewith War Diary for
71st Bde R.F.A. for month
of September 1915

Nicholson
[signature]
for Lt Col [?]
O in c 71st Bde R.F.A.

30/9/15

CONFIDENTIAL.

W A R D I A R Y

of

71st Brigade R.F.A.

(volume 38)

From 1st September 1918. To 30th September 1918.

WAR DIARY or INTELLIGENCE SUMMARY

Army Form C. 2118.

9 S L 37

Place	Date	Hour	Summary of Events and Information	Remarks and references to Appendices
VIS-EN-ARTOIS	1-2/9/18		Day spent carrying ammunition & arranging for the attack the following day.	
	2/9/18		Guns in support of 2nd Canadian Brigade, covering the infantry, moved North of the Cambrai road in the neighbourhood of BOIRY NOTRE DAME to cover the flank which rested on the SCARPE(?).	
	3/9/18		Registration carried out. Hostile artillery fairly quiet, all the fire coming from the neighbourhood of VITRY.	
	4/9/18		In support(?) MONCHY, in front of(?) the march(?) of(?) Hd. qts. Both old British support line before the march(?) is DEAD	
	5/9/18		Head quarters moved back to the old British support lines in ARRAS, batteries Relieved by the 261 Bde. Spent the night in ARRAS.	
	6/9/18	10.15am	MAN'S corner. Orders from Divn. to Person arrives at 3.30 p.m.	
	7/9/18		One section of 13. C. D. & the whole of A/71 relieves sections of 38/Bde.	
	8/9/18		Relief completed. HQ in HAZINGARBE.	
HAZINGARBE	9/9/18		Registration was carried out during the day by 18pdr & 4.5″ How. Hostile artillery very quiet. Harassing fire carried out during the night.	A
	10/9/18		Hostile artillery very quiet. Night harassing fire carried out. Movement observed & dispersed.	A

Army Form C. 2118.

WAR DIARY
or
INTELLIGENCE SUMMARY.
(Erase heading not required.)

Instructions regarding War Diaries and Intelligence Summaries are contained in F. S. Regs., Part II. and the Staff Manual respectively. Title pages will be prepared in manuscript.

Place	Date	Hour	Summary of Events and Information	Remarks and references to Appendices
MAZINGARBE	11/9/18	8pm	Wireless call received & counter Battery shoot carried out. Movement seen & disposed. A number of trains observed on PROVIN Line. Hostile artillery wizening	
	12/9/18		Registration was carried out by 18Pdrs during the day. Enemy artillery normal. Harassing fire carried out during the night by 18Pdrs & 4.5 Hows.	
	13/9/18		Hostile artillery slightly above normal. Considerable movement seen & fired on	
	14/9/18	6am-6.28am	Barrage by 18Pdrs & 4.5 Hows was put down in support of Minor Operations. Hostile artillery more active. Harassing fire carried out during the night.	
	15/9/18	5.30am 5.45am 5.55am 12 noon 4pm 4pm-6.30pm	GHOSTLY. GREASE & GAMBIT trenches bombarded by 18Pdrs at request of Infantry, 540 Rds fired Barrage was put down in support of operations by left Div. Group Trenches bombarded at above rate of fire in preparation of Infantry attack Barrage fired & support of Infantry Operations Hostile artillery above normal	
	16/9/18	6am-6.30am 4am-6am	"C" Battery Position Gassed with 5.9", 4.2 Gas shells. 110/9/310/Rds GHOSTLY, GREASE, GAMBIT trench fired on at request of Infantry. Hostile artillery above normal	
	17/9/18	4.5p-	Barrage was fired & support of Minor operations. 2340 Rds 18Pr & 450 4.5 Hows Hostile artillery normal "C" Battery Position Gassed with Yellow & Green X shells. 5.9", 4.2". A D.R. of movement & general position during the day.	
	18/9/18	3.45am	"C" Battery Position again Gassed. Guns were moved out. The enemy to unforced position. Harassing fire carried out during the night. Hostile artillery normal. Enemy artillery fired 200 rounds in vicinity of "B" battery, 4.2" at least 50% were "DUDS"	

WAR DIARY or INTELLIGENCE SUMMARY

Army Form C. 2118.

Place	Date	Hour	Summary of Events and Information	Remarks and references to Appendices
MAZINGARBE	19/9/18	24dpm	HULL & HAMLET Trenches were bombarded with 100 rounds of 4.5" How a/c issues 17/15. Infantry. A Co. of movement was observed during the day & about 150 Rounds expended by "B" Battery in engaging it. Harassing fire was carried out during the night on Trench Revets, Tramways & hence junctions. Expenditure 200 Rds 18pdr. 100Rds 4.5"How. Gun flashes were observed at different points during the day – necessary retaliation made.	J
	20/9/18	9.50 am	Enemy put down a Barrage between QUARRIES & The DUMP. 18pdr & 4.5 How retaliated on GHOSTLY, GAMBIT & GREASE Trenches. Very little movement observed. Enemy artillery otherwise quiet during the day. 4.5 Hows registered during today. A new position further NORTH, was reconnoitred for C Battery.	J
	21/9/18		Hostile artillery very quiet – Throughout the day Movement below normal. Harassing fire from 10pm until 1am – 200 Rds. 18pdr + 100 Rds. 4.5 How was carried out during the night. From 10pm heavy shelled with 4.2" every morning. A Battery forward gun was fired on.	J
	22/9/18	8 pm.	Enemy artillery above normal. A good deal of movement was observed & fired on. Our front was extended STH NORTH & two 18pdr Batteries of the 158th Bde RFA (Q+D) came under the Tactical Command of the Outre Sub: Group between 3am & 6am 300 Rds 18pdr. Harassing fire was carried out on hostile Trenches etc between 9pm at visual of Tk Infantry.	J
		9.30-12.4pm	Harassed COPPER TRENCH with 50 Rds 18pdr at visual of tk Infantry.	
	23/9/18	3.30pm	Hostile artillery normal during the day. Much movement seen & engaged. A "Chinese" Barrage was put down in support of a fan attack. Ammunition expended. 300 Rds 18pdr	J
		16.30 Rpd 270 4.5How. Harassing fire was carried out between 9pm & midnight. 100 W.S. New wagon lines were reconnoitred at BARLIN.		

WAR DIARY or INTELLIGENCE SUMMARY

Army Form C. 2118.

(Erase heading not required.)

Place	Date	Hour	Summary of Events and Information	Remarks and references to Appendices
MAZINGARBE	24/9/16		A Quiet day. Water lines of all Batteries and HQ moved from HERSIN to BARLIN. "D" Battery carried out a registration shoot with aeroplane observation. Expending 70 rounds. A Barrage of the Infantry at the junction of GHOSTLY & GAMBIT Trenches was turned on. 12 rounds H.E.S. Hour. Movement during the day below normal. Usual harassing fire carried out during the night.	✓
	25/9/16		A very Quiet day. Movement much below normal. Hostile artillery very Quiet. A Heavy Barrage was put down by Artillery on our left. Usual harassing fire was carried out between 9pm & midnight.	✓
	26/9/16		A very Quiet day. Movement below normal except 11.30 am & 2.30 pm our E.A. was brought down behind HULLUCH. Hi. harassing fire was carried out.	✓
	27/9		A Quiet day. A good deal of movement which was enjoyed by 18 pdrs.	✓
	28/9/16	pm	Throughout the day & night Vigorous harassing fire was carried out at selected localities. Contained as under for all Batteries. 800 A harassing 400 A × 120 A harassing 500 B.N.R.	✓
	29/9/16		Harassing fire was continued throughout day & night. Movement was engaged & 18 pdrs registration effected.	✓
	30/9		A Barrage lasting from 6.15 am until 6.30 am was put down in support of Infantry operations. Harassing fire was continued throughout the day & night. D/71 VU.18.PA fired 176 rounds B.N.C on selected targets. Movement was enjoyed during the day.	✓

3-8
1B Cornwall 8/71st. 13th R.F.A

CONFIDENTIAL.

War Diary

of

71st Bde R.F.A.

From 1/10/18 to 31/10/18

Volume 39.

WAR DIARY or INTELLIGENCE SUMMARY

Army Form C. 2118.

A/D 11/2 R.F.A.

October 1918

Place: In the Field at HQ G.17.b.93

Date	Hour	Summary of Events and Information	Remarks and references to Appendices
1/10		Quiet day. Hostile artillery inactive. Nothing special to report. Good weather. Visibility fair.	AB
2/10		An eventful day. At 4 a.m. the enemy commenced to withdraw to the HAUTE-DEULE CANAL. By 9 a.m. infantry had pushed forward patrols into the enemy support line. No enemy were encountered. At 9 a.m. one troop of WINGLES was blown up by enemy. By 10 a.m. the other two sections had taken up positions in the BROWN LINE also. By night fall Divisions were ordered forward to positions in G.30.b.55. there the whole Divisional front.	AB
	6 p.m.	A, B, C, D batteries were ordered forward to positions in G.30.b.55. there were in action before dawn 3/10/.	
3/10		Our troops continued to advance. By night fall Cates Bayonets had reached the line of railway running through WINGLES and the METALLURGIQUE WORKS M.G. above enemy positions between WINGLES and the Canal. B & D Batteries moved to positions in H.14.b. (between HULLOCH and BENIFONTAINE) and were in action by 3 a.m.	AB
4/10/18		A & C Batteries moved to forward positions. Targets were fired on during the day at the request of the Infantry & Harrasing fire was carried out during the night on roads East of the HAUTE DEULE CANAL.	A
5/10/18		A, B & D Batteries broke out Anti-personnel fires & sections from Heu main positions shelling targets were enemy retreating harrassing fire carried out on roads East of the Canal.	E

WAR DIARY
or
INTELLIGENCE SUMMARY.
(Erase heading not required.)

Army Form C. 2118.

Place	Date	Hour	Summary of Events and Information	Remarks and references to Appendices
G.17.b.9.3	6/10/18		D/71 Bde RFA moved one sniper gun to H4a5.3 Movement was engaged during 1st day. Harassing fire carried out during the night. German peace proposals launched.	
	7/10/18		D/71 Bde RFA moved another sniper gun to B14.a.5.3. Movement engaged harassing fire carried out during the night.	
	8/10/18		A quiet day although the enemy artillery slightly increased his activity. A good deal of movement was observed & engaged. Harassing fire was carried out during the night. Lieut. Col. C. M. INGHAM relinquished command of the Brigade on promotion to Brigadier General & assumed the 15th DIVISIONAL ARTILLERY vice Brig General E.B. Macnaghten DSO. 4 NF & GF calls were received during the day & 1st Angle fired on by 18 pdrs. L.IS. Horse movement above normal + engaged each time it was seen/heard. Harassing fire was carried out during the night.	
	9/10/18		A very quiet day. Usual harassing fire was carried out during the night.	
	10/10/18		The Brigade pulled out of the line with the exception of a section each of A,B & C Batteries + two sections of D Battery. Batteries moved to their respective	
PHILOSOPHE	11/10/18		billets lines.	
"	12/10/18		Day spent in cleaning up generally.	
"	13/10/18		Training commenced	
"	14/10/18		Training continued	
"	15/10/18		Sections of A,B & C Batteries in action at wagon hill returned. J.A.B r C 3-4175 D-4175. Section of D/71 renamed with 15 D-4/75 in action.	
MEURCHIN	16/10/18		Brigade moved forward. Bde advanced in winning echelon to FOSSE 5. W.J. CARVIN 21 gun dust fell fell reflecting on CARVIN. MEURCHIN. Our artillery although in action did not fire.	

WAR DIARY or INTELLIGENCE SUMMARY

Army Form C. 2118.

WO/4 7th R.I.R.

October 1918.

Place	Date	Hour	Summary of Events and Information	Remarks and references to Appendices
ENNECOURT	17/10/18		Bn moved in evening to ENNECOURT. Billets vanguard. A Coy & HQ Coy in neighbourhood of Bn.	A57
MARTINVAL	18/10/18		Bn moved forward to LA NEUVILLE. Halting for a few hours, then on to MARTINVAL. Billets received patrols in huts, officers billeted with open fires.	A57
La CAPELLE	19/10/18		Bn moved forward to CHATEAU BLOCU - came into action and at midday advanced to LA CAPELLE. One other Bn BM. advanced with 15th and supported did not first owing to the barrage of hostile civilians. 46, 23 & 13th R.I.R. 45th I.B. and 7th & R.R.I.R. became the reserve of the Bn. 46, 23 & 13th R.I.R. going in advance with 46, 23, & 158 Bn A.I. in support.	A57
GENECH	20/10/18		Moved to CHATEAU GENECH with 45th I.B. - in Bois de GENECH.	A57
LA GLANERIE	21/10/18		Moved to LA GLANERIE with 45 I.B.	A57
"	22/10/18		Got rest - cleaning up generally.	A57
RUE D'HOTEL	23/10/18		Moved to RUE D'HOTEL. 45th I.B. remaining at LA GLANERIE	A57
"	24/10/18		At rest at Rue d'Hotel.	A57
"	25/10/18		Lieut Col T CARLYON DSO arrived from 5/9 Bn and took over command of Bn. Major ROWDEN returning to 6/7th.	A57
"	26/10/18		Training commenced	A57
"	27/10/18		Training continued	A57

Army Form C. 2118.

WAR DIARY
or
INTELLIGENCE SUMMARY.
(Erase heading not required.)

October 1918.   N31 1 B 4 R 17

Instructions regarding War Diaries and Intelligence Summaries are contained in F. S. Regs., Part II. and the Staff Manual respectively. Title pages will be prepared in manuscript.

Place	Date	Hour	Summary of Events and Information	Remarks and references to Appendices
Reed H57E6	28/10/18		Training continued	
"	29/10/18		" "	
"	30/10/18		" "	
"	31/10/18		" "	

T. Colyer de Col.
LT. COL. R.F.A.
COMMANDING 71st BRIGADE, R.F.A.
31-10-18

CONFIDENTIAL.

WAR DIARY.

of

71st Brigade R.F.A.

(Volume 40).

From 1st November 1918.   To 30th November 1918.

WAR DIARY or INTELLIGENCE SUMMARY

Army Form C. 2118.

HQ 71st Bde RFA

November 1916

Place	Date	Hour	Summary of Events and Information	Remarks and references to Appendices
Rue d'Hôtel	1/11/16		At rest. Training continued.	
"	2/11/16, 3/11/16, 4/11/16		" " "	
"	5/11/16		Activity was reported of the SCHELDTE by 58 Divn on our Right. 15 Bn on our left. DHI moved forward to the junction to ASSIST - with orders of 71 C.O. 71st Bde RFA	
PETIT RUMES	9/11/16		Bde moved forward to PETIT RUMES. DHI remained at position returned to Y. "B" for tactical purposes. Bde together with 45th DB moved across R. SCHELDTE via ANTOINE to BRAFFE	
BRAFFE	10/11/16		Bde moving to AUBECHIES. Armistice signed. Hostilities ceased at 1100	
AUBECHIES	11/11/16		at rest.	
"	12/11/16		Training recommenced	
"	13/11/16		Training continued. 15 Bn has joined from 1 Corps 5 Army to 3 Corps	
"	14/11/16		2nd ARMY, for the purpose of advancing with that Army into Germany.	
"	15/11/16 to 30/11/16		Training and Sports and education continued.	

30/11/16

T. Colyer Lt. Col. R.F.A.
O.C. 71st Bde. R.F.A.

CONFIDENTIAL.

WAR DIARY

of

71st Brigade R.F.A.

(Volume 41.)

From 1st December 1918. To 31st December 1918.

Army Form C. 2118.

WAR DIARY
or
INTELLIGENCE SUMMARY.

(Erase heading not required.)

December 1918. HQ 71 B'de RFA

Place	Date	Hour	Summary of Events and Information	Remarks and references to Appendices
AUBECHIES	Dec 1		Education and training continued	
CHAPELLE A OIE	" 2		B'de HQ moved to CHAPELLE A OIE	
"	" 3		Education and training continued	
"	" 4		Education and training continued. B/H moved from AUBECHIES to CHAPELLE a OIE	
"	" 5		" " "	
"	" 6		" " "	
"	" 7		71 B RFA sent 100 Officers and OR's to line the road near TOURPET on the occasion of a visit by HM King GEORGE V	
"	" 8 to " 15		Education and training continued	
CHIEVRES	" 16		Brigade moved to CHIEVRES en route for a new area	
HORRUES	" 17		Brigade moved on to HORRUES	
REBECQ-ROGNON	" 18		Brigade moved to REBECQ-ROGNON	
"	" 19		Brigade remained in REBECQ-ROGNON area - cleaning up	
"	"20 to "31		Brigade remained in REBECQ-ROGNON area. During the month 50 men have been demobilised	

24/12/18

T. Colyer
LT. COL. R.F.A.
COMMANDING 71st BRIGADE R.F.A.

CONFIDENTIAL.

WAR DIARY.

of

71st Brigade R.F.A.

(Volume 42)

From 1st January 1919.   To 31st January 1919.

Army Form C. 2118.

WAR DIARY
or
INTELLIGENCE SUMMARY.

(Erase heading not required.) HQ 91B RFA

January 1919.

Place	Date	Hour	Summary of Events and Information	Remarks and references to Appendices
R Berra Pognon	1/1/19		Education and demobilization continued.	
"	31/1/19			

T. Canyon to Lt. RFA
O.C. 91 Bde. RFA.

31/1/19

CONFIDENTIAL.

WAR DIARY

of

71st Brigade R.F.A.

(Volume 43)

From 1st February 1919.   To 28th February 1919.

WAR DIARY
or
INTELLIGENCE SUMMARY. HQ 71 Bde RFA

Army Form C. 2118.

February 1919

WO 95/1522 RFA

Place	Date	Hour	Summary of Events and Information	Remarks and references to Appendices
Rebecq-Rognon	1/2/19 to 28/2/19		Education and demobilization continued.	

T. Cowper Lt. Col. RFA
O.C. 71 Bde RFA

CONFIDENTIAL.

WAR DIARY

of

71st Brigade R.F.A.

(Volume 44.)

From 1st March 1919.   To 31st March 1919.

WAR DIARY
or
INTELLIGENCE SUMMARY.

Army Form C. 2118.

HQrs 71 Bde RFA. March 1919

Place	Date	Hour	Summary of Events and Information	Remarks and references to Appendices
REFFCQ - ROGNON	1/3/19 31/3/19		Demobilization and reduction to cadre continued.	MM 4 3

A May Capt
for A. Col RFA
Comdg. 71st Bde RFA.

CONFIDENTIAL.

WAR DIARY

of.

71st Brigade R.F.A.

(Volume 45)

From 1st April 1919.   To 30th April 1919.

Army Form C. 2118.

WAR DIARY
or
INTELLIGENCE SUMMARY.

(Erase heading not required.)

April 1919   71st Bde R.F.A.

Place	Date	Hour	Summary of Events and Information	Remarks and references to Appendices
Petney - Roquen	1/4/19 to 6/4/19		Demobilization a reduction to cadre continued. All Brigade horses have been sent away. Two drafts have been sent to Army of occupation (2nd Army).	

T. Carter
LT. COL. R.F.A.
COMMANDING 71st BRIGADE, R.F.A.

Army Form C. 2113.

WAR DIARY
or
INTELLIGENCE SUMMARY.
(Erase heading not required.)

71 Bde RFA Appx 45

Place	Date	Hour	Summary of Events and Information	Remarks and references to Appendices
REBECQ	1/5/19 to 31/5/19		Demobilization instruction to cases continued. All ranks off men volunteers have been sent to lu RHINE	

C W Naylor Capt
for
LT. COL. R.F.A.
COMMANDING 71st BRIGADE, R.F.A.

www.ingramcontent.com/pod-product-compliance
Lightning Source LLC
Chambersburg PA
CBHW080847230426
43662CB00013B/2044